REDISCOVERING THE
CHRISTIAN FEASTS

REDISCOVERING THE CHRISTIAN FEASTS

A Study in the Services of the Christian Year

Robert E. Webber

The Alleluia! Series of the Institute for Worship Studies

Hendrickson Publishers, Inc.
P. O. Box 3473
Peabody, Massachusetts 01961-3473

REDISCOVERING THE CHRISTIAN FEASTS:
A *Study in the Services of the Christian Year*
by Robert E. Webber

ISBN 1-56563-276-1

First printing, January 1998

Printed in the United States of America

CONTENTS

WELCOME TO THE
ALLELUIA! SERIES

This Bible study series has been designed by the Institute for Worship Studies primarily for laypersons in the church.

We are living in a time when worship has become a distinct priority for the church. For years, the church has emphasized evangelism, teaching, fellowship, missions, and service to society to the neglect of the very source of its power—worship. But in recent years we have witnessed a Spirit-led renewed interest in and practice of worship.

Because worship has been neglected for so many years, there is precious little information and teaching on the subject in our seminaries, Bible schools, and local churches.

The mission of the Institute for Worship Studies is to make the study of worship available to everyone in the church—academician, pastor, worship leader, music minister, and layperson.

Laypersons will find the seven courses of the Alleluia! Series to be inspiring, informative, and life changing. Each course of study is rooted in biblical teaching, draws from the rich historical treasures of the church, and is highly practical and accessible.

The Institute for Worship Studies presents this course, *Rediscovering the Christian Feasts: A Study in the Services of the Christian Year,* as a service to the local church and to its ministry of worship to God. May this study warm your heart, inform your mind, and kindle your spirit. May it inspire and set on fire the worship of the local church. And may this study minister to the church and to the One, Holy, Triune God in whose name it is offered.

THE SEVEN COURSES IN THE ALLELUIA! WORSHIP SERIES

Learning to Worship with All Your Heart: A Study in the Biblical Foundations of Worship

You are led into the rich teachings of worship in both the Old and the New Testaments. Learn the vocabulary of worship, be introduced to theological themes, and study various descriptions of worship. Each lesson inspires you to worship at a deeper level—from the inside out.

Rediscovering the Missing Jewel: A Study of Worship through the Centuries
This stretching course introduces you to the actual worship styles of Christians in other centuries and geographical locations. Study the history of the early, medieval, Reformation, modern, and contemporary periods of worship. Learn from them how your worship today may be enriched, inspired, and renewed. Each lesson introduces you to rich treasures of worship adaptable for contemporary use.

Renew Your Worship! A Study in the Blending of Traditional and Contemporary Worship
This inspiring course leads you into a deeper understanding and experience of your Sunday worship. How does worship bring the congregation into the presence of God, mold the people by the Word, and feed the believers spiritually? The answer to these and other questions will bring a new spiritual depth to our experience of worship.

Enter His Courts with Praise: A Study of the Role of Music and the Arts in Worship
This course introduces you to the powerful way the arts can communicate the mystery of God at work in worship. Music, visual arts, drama, dance, and mime are seen as means through with the gospel challenges the congregation and changes lives.

Rediscovering the Christian Feasts: A Study in the Services of the Christian Year
This stimulating and stretching course helps you experience the traditional church calendar with new eyes. It challenges the secular concept of time and shows how the practice of the Christian year offers an alternative to secularism and shapes the Christian's day-to-day experience of time, using the gospel as its grid.

Encountering the Healing Power of God: A Study in the Sacred Actions of Worship
This course makes a powerful plea for the recovery of those sacred actions that shape the spiritual life. Baptism, Communion, anointing with oil, and other sacred actions are all interpreted with reflection on the death and resurrection of Jesus. These actions shape the believer's spiritual experience into a continual pattern of death to sin and rising to life in the Spirit.

Empowered by the Holy Spirit: A Study in the Ministries of Worship
This course will challenge you to see the relationship between worship and life in the secular world. It empowers the believer in evangelism, spiritual formation, social action, care ministries, and other acts of love and charity.

Take all seven coursesand earn a Certificate of Worship Studies (CWS). For more information, call the Institute for Worship Studies at (630) 510-8905.

INTRODUCTION

Redicovering the Christian Feasts: A Study in the Services of the Christian Year may be used for personal study or a small-group course of study and spiritual formation. It is designed around thirteen easy-to-understand sessions. Each session has a two-part study guide. The first part is an individual study that each person completes privately. The second part is a one-hour interaction and application session that group members complete together (during the week or in an adult Sunday school setting). The first part helps you recall and reflect on what you've read, while the small-group study applies the material to each member's personal life and experience of public worship.

Rediscovering the Christian Feasts is designed for use by one or more people. When the course is used in a group setting, the person who is designated as the leader simply needs to lead the group through the lesson step by step. It is always best to choose a leader before you begin.

Here are some suggestions for making your group discussions lively and insightful.

SUGGESTIONS FOR THE STUDENT

A few simple guidelines will help you use the study guide most effectively. They can be summarized under three headings: Prepare, Participate, and Apply.

Prepare

1. Answer each question in the study guide, "Part I: Personal Study," thoughtfully and critically.

2. Do all your work prayerfully. Prayer itself is worship. As you increase your knowledge of worship, do so in a spirit of prayerful openness before God.

Participate

1. Don't be afraid to ask questions. Your questions may give voice to the other members in the group. Your courage in speaking out will give others permission to talk and may encourage more stimulating discussion.

2. Don't hesitate to share your personal experiences. Abstract thinking has its place, but personal illustrations will help you and others remember the material more vividly.

3. Be open to others. Listen to the stories that other members tell, and respond to them in a way that does not invalidate their experiences.

Apply

1. Always ask yourself, "How can this apply to worship?"

2. Commit yourself to being a more intentional worshiper. Involve yourself in what is happening around you.

3. Determine your gifts. Ask yourself, "What can I do in worship that will minister to the body of Christ?" Then offer your gifts and talents to worship.

SUGGESTIONS FOR THE LEADER

Like the worship that it advocates, the group study in *Rediscovering the Christian Feasts* is dialogic in nature. Because this study has been developed around the principles of discussion and sharing, a monologue or lecture approach will not work. The following guidelines will help you encourage discussion, facilitate learning, and implement the practice of worship. Use these guidelines with "Part II: Group Discussion" in each session.

1. Encourage the participants to prepare thoroughly and to bring their Bibles and study guides to each session.

2. Begin each session with prayer. Since worship is a kind of prayer, learning about worship should be a prayerful experience.

3. Discuss each question individually. Ask for several answers and encourage people to react to comments made by others.

4. Use a chalkboard or flip chart or dry-erase board. Draw charts and symbols that visually enhance the ideas being presented. Outline major concepts.

5. Look for practical applications of answers and suggestions that are offered. Try asking questions like, "How would you include this in our worship?" "How would you feel about that change?" "How does this insight help you to be a better worshiper?"

6. Invite concrete personal illustrations. Ask questions like, "Have you experienced that? Where? When? Describe how you felt in that particular situation."

7. When you have concluded Session 13, send the names and addresses of all the students who will complete the class to: Institute for Worship Studies, Box 894, Wheaton, IL 60189. We will then send a certificate of accomplishment for each student in time for you to distribute them during the last class. The cost of each certificate is $1.00. (Add $3.00 for postage and handling.)

One final suggestion: Purchase the larger work upon which this course is based, volume 5 of *The Complete Library of Christian Worship*. This volume, entitled *The Services of the Christian Year*, is a beautiful 8½-by-11-inch coffee table book that will inform your mind and inspire your heart through hours of reading and study.

PART I

THE CYCLE

OF LIGHT

MARKING TIME

A Study in the Christian View of Time

I recently visited Stonehenge, the site of mysterious megaliths in England. These huge stones (some of them up to one ton in weight) are arranged in a series of concentric circles in the beautiful farmland of England.

Interpreters of history argue that a prehistoric civilization once lived there on the great plains, of which Stonehenge was apparently a center. But no one is absolutely certain about the function of those mysteriously placed stones. One interesting explanation is that the stones mark time. They are placed in such a way that the light of the sun moves around the circle through each month of the year.

Whether or not the stones' primary purpose was marking time, no one knows for certain. But their presence point out that all people have ways to mark time. We all live by a yearly calendar that marks time from January to December. Many of us also mark time by an academic calendar that runs from September to June. We all have personal calendars in that mark time by special events such as marriages and births.

THE BIBLICAL WAY OF MARKING TIME

In the Scripture time is marked by God's saving events. An event time is called *kairos* (from which we get our word *crisis*). The time between kairos events is called *chronos* (from which we get our word *chronology*).

The scriptural concept of time is obviously rooted in the Christ event as the primary kairos, or crisis time. The Christ event is the extraordinary time toward which all time moves and from which all time proceeds. I like to think of the picture of an hourglass on its side. The Christ event, of course, is the middle. Everything else gathers around it.

We speak of the Christ event and its relation to time in the following three ways:

- The Christ event is fulfilled time. In the Christ event the Old Testament expectation of the Messiah is fulfilled. Jesus himself said, "The time has come. . . . The kingdom of God is near. Repent and believe the good news!" (Mark 1:15). (See Peter's sermon on the day of Pentecost, Acts 2:14–36.)
- The Christ event is the time of salvation. The Christ event is that moment in time when God dethroned the powers and established salvation and healing for the world (see Col 2:15).
- The Christ event introduces anticipatory time. We live in the time between the cross and the disarming of the powers on the one hand, and the second coming and the destruction of the powers on the other. Consequently, Christians live in hope of the future, awaiting the final judgment on evil.

THE CHRISTIAN YEAR

In order to understand the Christian year, we need to recognize that it is the Christian way of marking time, which is based on the kairos moments of God's action in history.

Christian time revolves around three important aspects of the Christ event:

- The birth of Christ: Advent, Christmas, and Epiphany are all related to the time of Christ's birth.
- The death and resurrection of Christ: Lent, Holy Week, and Easter mark these primary events of salvation.
- Pentecost and the second coming: Pentecost marks the coming of the Holy Spirit, the beginning of the church, and the expectation of the return of Jesus.

THE MEANING OF EACH SEASON

Let's get better acquainted with the Christian year by looking more closely at each season.

THE CYCLE OF LIGHT

The seasons of Advent, Christmas, and Epiphany relate to the coming of Christ, the Light of the World (see John 1:1–9). These three seasons are called the cycle of light because they focus on Christ, the Light of the World.

Advent

The word *Advent* means "coming." It signifies the period preceding the birth of Christ when the church anticipates the coming of the Messiah (see Isa 11:1–10). Today more and more Christians are recovering Advent because of the spiritual meaning it gives to Christmas in the face of a strong anti-Christian cultural bias, as well as the materialistic secularization of Christmas.

Christmas

Christmas celebrates the birth of Christ and the incarnation of God among us (see Luke 2:1–14). The real meaning of Christmas tends to get lost in the secular hoopla that surrounds this great saving event. The church is seeking to do more to emphasize its spiritual meaning.

Epiphany

The word *Epiphany* means "manifestation." It refers to Jesus' being manifested to the world as Messiah, Son of God, Savior of the World. The Epiphany is always commemorated on January 6 (the end of the twelve days of Christmas) and celebrates the coming of the Magi to pay homage to Jesus (see Matt 2:1–12).

THE CYCLE OF LIFE

The second cycle of the Christian year includes Lent, Holy Week, and Easter. It ends on Pentecost day. This is frequently called the cycle of life because it recalls Jesus' death and resurrection (see John 15:18–25).

Lent

Lent is a Latin word that means "spring." The spiritual meaning given to the word is preparation. During Lent we prepare with Jesus to move toward his death. This is why the notion of giving something up or taking on a spiritual discipline has become a central part of the Lenten spiritual journey.

Lent lasts forty days in keeping with the symbolic meaning of that number forty. Moses spent forty years in the wilderness. Jesus spent forty days in the desert. In each case the sense of spiritual preparation for the task that lies ahead is central (see Matt 4:1–11). During the forty days preceding the death of Jesus, we prepare to accompany him in his death.

Holy Week

During Holy Week the church enacts the final events that lead up to the crucifixion of Jesus. Holy Week originated in Jerusalem, where Christians marked the locations of the final events in Jesus' life. (Today the stations of the cross pilgrimage repeats the ancient road to the cross.) The final week begins with Palm Sunday and ends with what is called the Great Triduum (the three great days). These days are Maundy Thursday, Good Friday, and the great paschal vigil of Saturday night that ends in the Easter celebration (see Mark 14–16).

Easter

Easter celebrates the resurrection of Jesus from the dead and all that the resurrection implies (see 1 Cor 15:20–28). Many churches are beginning to recover the ancient practice of celebrating Easter for fifty days, culminating in the coming of the Holy Spirit at Pentecost.

Pentecost and after Pentecost

Pentecost Sunday ends Easter and begins the third season, which stretches from Pentecost to Christ the King Sunday, the final Sunday before the first Sunday of Advent when the cycle of light begins again.

This third period of time is called Ordinary Time because no saving events are celebrated after Pentecost. However, every Sunday is a celebration of Jesus' death and resurrection. In this sense every Sunday is a "little Easter." Pentecost season recalls the events of the church, its origins, and its growth. As Pentecost ends, the church turns its attention toward the anticipation of the second coming of Christ. This is why the season after Pentecost ends with the Christ the King Sunday.

CONCLUSION

Let's conclude our introduction to the Christian year by looking at the cycle of the entire year from a Christian perspective. Here it is:

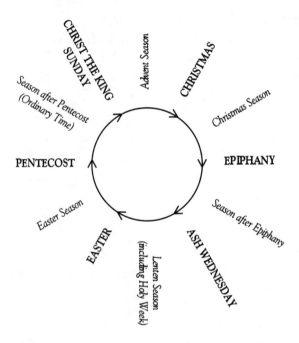

This cycle remembers and proclaims the Christ event and anticipates the new heavens and the new earth. If your church does not practice the Christian year, it can begin now. The Christian year has the power to shape your worship life around Jesus and his saving events.

STUDY GUIDE

Read Session 1, "Marking Time,"
before starting the study guide.

PART I: PERSONAL STUDY

Complete the following questions individually.

1. *Life Connection*

◆ How do you mark time? Most of us mark time by crisis events, such as birth, marriage, and death. Is there a significant event in your life that represents a turning point for you—a new point by which to mark time? Tell about that event. _____

_____

_____

_____

2. *Content Questions*

◆ How do the Scriptures mark time? _____

_____

_____

◆ Read Exodus 12:1–29. How does this passage illustrate the scriptural way of marking time for Israel? _____

_____

_____

◆ Read Luke 23:44–49. How does this passage express the defining moment for the Christian way of marking time? _____

_____

_____

◆ Read John 1:1–14. How does this passage speak to us of the Christian way of marking time? _____

_____

◆ How do Christmas and Easter shape your way of marking time?

_____

_____

◆ In your own words explain how the Christ event shapes the following views of time:

a. The Christ event as *fulfilled time* _____

_____

_____

b. The Christ event as *the time of salvation* _____

_____

_____

c. The Christ event as *anticipatory time* _____

_____

_____

◆ State and describe the three events around which Christian time is organized.

a. _____

b. _____

c. _____

◆ Briefly describe the meaning of each season of Christian time.

Advent _____

_____

Christmas _____

_____

Epiphany _____

_____

Lent _____

_____

Holy Week _____

_____

Easter _____

_____

After Pentecost _____

_____

◆ Briefly describe the distinction between the cycle of light and the cycle of life.

Cycle of light _____

_____

Cycle of life _____

_____

3. *Application*

◆ How would you like to *allow* the Christian year to organize your spiritual journey through the year? Think about it for awhile and then write out your answer. _____

_____

_____

_____

PART II: GROUP DISCUSSION

The following questions are designed for group discussion. Share the insights you gained from your personal study in Part I.

Write out all answers that group members give to the questions on a chalkboard, a flip chart, or a dry erase board.

1. *Life Connection*

◆ Begin the discussion by asking various group members to share the crisis events by which their lives are marked.

2. *Thought Questions*

◆ Read Exodus 12:1–29 and comment on the many references in this passage to "remembering the event." Has anyone in this group attended a Jewish Passover? Comment on how Passover remembers the Exodus event.

◆ Read Luke 23:44–49. Ask, "How does the death and resurrection of Christ order the way we mark church time week by week and year by year?" "In what special ways do we mark Jesus' death and resurrection?"

- Read John 1:1–14. Ask, "How does the incarnation shape the way we mark time here at the church?" "What are the *special* things we do during this season to set it apart?"

- Compare the answers given above to the three ways the Christ event marks time. Discuss each Scripture.
Fulfilled time: Acts 2:14–36
The Time of Salvation: Colossians 2:15
Anticipatory Time: Mark 5:8

- Walk through the Christian year talking about the meaning of each season. Write out people's comments.

3. *Application*

- Evaluate the way your church marks time. Is the dominant approach a Christian way of marking time, an academic way, or a civil way?

- It has been said that "the Christian year orders and organizes congregational spirituality." How does that happen at your church?

- Which season of the year best describes the personality of your church? Is it an Advent church? Christmas church? Epiphany church? Lenten church? Holy Week church? Easter church? Pentecost church?

- How could your church emphasize the many moods of the Christian year?

LONGING FOR THE MESSIAH

A Study in Advent

We are having some landscaping done around our house, so we recently met with the landscaper to go over the plans.

Before the landscaper would show us the plans, he said he had to make something clear. "I won't," he said, "have time to do the work until after July 15."

"Oh, no!" said my wife. "Bob doesn't like to wait. He wants everything done yesterday."

I am going to wait. But I think most of us, like myself, don't like to wait.

Advent, however, is all about waiting. Waiting for the Messiah to come and waiting for the fulfillment of Jesus' work in the new heavens and the new earth—a kind of double waiting.

THE BIBLICAL BASIS OF ADVENT

Advent is associated with three themes:

- The coming of the Messiah. Israel waited and longed for the coming of the Messiah. The Old Testament is filled with passages of prophetic utterance that express the longing for a new day (see, for example, Isa 2:1–5; 7:10–16; 11:1–10; 35:1–10).

- The birth of Christ, not only in Bethlehem but also in our hearts. A unique characteristic of Jesus is that he not only comes into history but also takes up residence within our hearts. Advent is a time to examine the presence of Jesus in our lives and to surrender our lives to him.

- The coming of Jesus at the end of history. The observance of Advent starts with an expectation of the second coming and then moves toward the first coming.

THE SPIRITUAL JOURNEY OF ADVENT

During the four weeks preceding Christmas, the church actually makes a spiritual journey—a pilgrimage into the birth of Christ. This journey is ordered by its worship.

We begin at a distance from the coming of Christ in Bethlehem, and each week we draw closer to the birth. Therefore worship during the first two weeks emphasizes the second coming of Christ and our need to prepare for his return.

The preparations we make for the second coming of Christ are similar to the preparations Israel made for the coming of the Messiah. Terms such as *hope, eager anticipation, longing,* and *looking toward the day* all express the kind of feelings Israel had as it waited for the Messiah. Those descriptive terms likewise capture the feelings we Christians have as we await the consummation of history and the redemption of all things.

But readiness is more than a feeling. It includes moral and spiritual preparation, the kind alluded to by Peter when he wrote, "What manner of persons ought you to be in holy conduct and godliness . . . ?" (2 Pet 3:11 NKJV). Consequently, a life of godly conduct is emphasized in the Scripture readings of the first two weeks of Advent.

Starting with the third week of Advent, the emphasis shifts to the feeling of joy. Since the day of his appearing is coming closer, the accent falls on what Christ will do in his coming. Both his first and second comings are related to salvation, redemption, and the renewal of Creation, which includes the restoration of all things to the Father and the sure destruction of evil. Since the overthrow of the devil and the kingdom of darkness will be a joyful event, the Scriptures, antiphons, hymns, prayers, and instruction of the third week all express this joy.

In the fourth week of Advent, we are brought closer to the event of Jesus' birth. Consequently, the emphasis of worship falls on the incarnation: God with us. In this service we are drawn up into the rejoicing of those immediately involved in the events surrounding the miraculous conception of Jesus Christ. We listen or sing together the Annunciation of the angel to Mary and Mary's great response, the Magnificat. These readings, together with the prayers and antiphons, bring us closer to Christ and increase our anticipation of his birth.

IDEAS FOR ADVENT WORSHIP

Advent breaks into the long Pentecost season with the dramatic announcement of the second coming of Jesus. This radical new message with its call to repentance and its high sense of expectancy demands high drama. An Advent full of color and bursting with drama and appropriate symbols will serve the meaning of Advent and ready the people for the second coming of Christ and for the birth of the Son. There are ways to convey the joyous anticipation:

♦ Change your worship environment for Advent. Traditionally churches are "greened" during Advent. Some churches green the sanctuary at the beginning of Advent, while other churches wait until the third week of Advent.

♦ Plan special services that feature Scripture readings and music appropriate to Advent. For example, celebrate the traditional service of nine lessons and carols.

♦ Do not neglect the penitential character of Advent. The entrance rites during Advent may express the sobriety of repentance. For example, sing or say the canticle Benedictus (see Luke 1:68–79) or sing praise and worship music that fits the theme of repentance.

♦ As part of the entrance rites, use the service for the lighting of the Advent wreath. The wreath should have four candles plus one in the middle. Light a candle each Sunday and conclude with the Christ candle (the fifth and middle candle) on Christmas Eve. The Advent candles express a sense of drama and expectancy.

♦ Observe Gaudete Sunday, the Sunday of joy. This is the third Sunday of Advent. The term *Gaudete* means "rejoice" and comes from the antiphon of the introit psalm "rejoice in the Lord always" (Phil 4:4). Gaudete Sunday is the most festive of the four Sundays of Advent. It is also the Sunday that proclaims the Virgin Mary as the bearer of God's Son. A rose may be placed in an obvious place as the symbol of Gaudete (joy) for the soon coming of Christ.

♦ Use Advent colors. The colors of Advent are royal purple or Sarum blue. Rose colors may be used on Gaudete Sunday. The deep colors express the penitential character of Advent. The rose color is more joyful and expresses the hope of the incarnation.

♦ Use drama to bring life to narrative portions of Scripture, such as John the Baptist's announcement of the coming of Christ.

♦ Sing Advent hymns and songs.

CONCLUSION

Worship during Advent can be a time of real spiritual renewal and commitment. Plan your worship so that it fulfills the themes of this traditional Advent prayer, taken from the Episcopal *Book of Common Prayer:*

Almighty God, give us grace to cast away the works of darkness, and put on the armor of light, now in the time of this mortal life in which your Son Jesus Christ came to visit us in great humility; that in the last day, when he shall come again in his glorious majesty to judge both the living and the dead, we may rise to the life immortal; through him who lives and reigns with you and the Holy Spirit, one God, now and for ever. *Amen.*

STUDY GUIDE

Read Session 2, "Longing for the Messiah,"
before starting the study guide.

PART I: PERSONAL STUDY

Complete the following questions individually.

1. *Life Connection*
- Do you remember a time when you waited and waited for something to happen . . . perhaps the birth of a child or the fulfillment of a dream or a vision? Describe your feelings of anticipation and the process of waiting.

_____

_____

_____

_____

_____

2. *Content Questions*
- What three themes are associated with Advent?
  a. _____

  b. _____

  c. _____

- What are the themes of the four Sundays of Advent? Summarize them in your own words.
First Sunday of Advent _____

_____

Second Sunday of Advent _____

_____

Third Sunday of Advent _____

_____

Fourth Sunday of Advent _____

_____

◆ Read the following Old Testament texts from Isaiah, which are appointed
for the four Sundays of Advent. Briefly explain how each one relates to
the theme of Advent waiting.
First Sunday, Isaiah 2:1–5: _____

_____

_____

Second Sunday, Isaiah 11:1–10: _____

_____

_____

Third Sunday, Isaiah 35:1–10: _____

_____

_____

Fourth Sunday, Isaiah 7:10–17: _____

_____

_____

◆ This session presents a number of ideas for use during Advent worship.
Write down the three that you would most like to see introduced into
the worship of your church.
a. _____
b. _____
c. _____

3. *Application*
◆ Pray the Advent prayer from the conclusion of this session. Pray it
slowly, thoughtfully, and with intention. What does this prayer say to
you? _____

_____

_____

_____

_____

PART II: GROUP DISCUSSION

The following questions are designed for group discussion. Share the insights you gained from your personal study in Part I.

Write out all answers that group members give to the questions on a chalkboard, a flip chart, or a dry erase board.

1. *Life Connection*

♦ Begin your discussion by asking group members to describe a time of waiting from their lives. Ask them to use words that describe their experience of waiting.

2. *Thought Questions*

♦ Discuss the three themes around which Advent is ordered. Look up the Scriptures and respond to each. (Read each text and ask people for insights.)

The Coming of the Messiah, Isaiah 2:1–5

The Birth of Christ in Bethlehem and in our hearts, John 3:1–17

The Coming of Jesus at the end of history, 1 Thessalonians 3:9–13

♦ Discuss the theme and mood of each of the four Sundays of Advent using the following texts. (Read each text and ask people for insights.)

First Sunday, Isaiah 2:1–5

Second Sunday, Isaiah 11:1–10

Third Sunday, Isaiah 35:1–10

Fourth Sunday, Isaiah 7:10–17

♦ Ask people to identify the three Advent worship ideas they would most like to see included in the worship of your church. Ask, "Why did you choose this aspect of Advent worship?" Look for several common themes in group members' responses.

3. *Application*

- Find bulletins from the previous Advent season. Discuss the strengths and weaknesses of the Advent celebration in one of those services.

- Identify some aspect of last year's celebration that could be used in your church in the next Advent season.

- Plan an Advent service. Choose hymns, songs, and prayers, and draw from the worship ideas presented in the text.

- Close by praying the prayer in the text from the *Book of Common Prayer*.

JOY TO THE WORLD

A Study in Christmas

 In the last lesson I confessed that I don't like to wait. I want everything to happen *now.*

I was also impatient as a little boy. My memories of Christmas morning are dominated by the waiting that I had to endure. It was our family tradition on Christmas morning to start with breakfast and then move into the living room to gather around the tree and the presents. Once we were around the tree, and in sight of all those presents that I had been rattling and shaking for the past week, my dad read the Christmas story from Luke 2 and prayed before we could open the presents.

Unfortunately for me, my father was long-winded. His Christmas prayer traveled through biblical history, encompassed the globe, remembered all the poor, and finally, after what seemed like hours of torture, ended with the amen. Then we were allowed to open our presents. But we had to open them one at a time in a slow turn around the family.

I always experienced a lot of joy in that event. Even though my joy came more from the presents and less from the birth of Jesus (I was a typical little boy), I can now reflect on that event and find more spiritual meaning in the joy. My guess is that your childhood experience is not significantly different from mine.

THE BIBLICAL BASIS FOR CHRISTMAS

The biblical basis for Christmas is found in the infancy narratives of Matthew and Luke. These narratives lend themselves to the kind of pageantry and celebration that has become common in Christmas worship. The accounts in Matthew and Luke provide us with different perspectives and themes.

- ◆ Matthew's Christmas theme. The Lord's messenger appears to Joseph in a dream and explains the meaning of the name *Jesus:* "He will save his people from their sins" (Matt 1:21). Matthew provides a theological interpretation of Jesus' birth and explains why Christ came.

- ◆ Luke's Christmas theme. Luke couches the announcement of Jesus' coming in the context of the oppressed. Joseph and Mary must pay taxes to the occupying power and, like most people, they found no room in the inn (see Luke 2:1–7).

The angelic announcement of the birth of the Savior of the world is made to poor shepherds watching their flock (Luke 2:8–20), not to the rich and famous.

The response to the good news is verbally expressed in the Magnificat (see Luke 1:46–55), the Song of Zechariah (see Luke 1:68–79), and the Gloria in Excelsis Deo of the angels (see Luke 2:14).

Luke shows us the hope that the birth of the Savior gives and provides us with the proper response to the salvation that comes through Jesus Christ.

THE PRACTICE OF CHRISTMAS WORSHIP

The Shape of Christmas Worship

The shape of worship during the Christmas season will follow the general order of worship (entrance, word, table, dismissal), each infused with the words, symbols, sounds, and sights of Christmas joy. As the worshiping congregation carefully plans and plays out these forms of worship, they will experience the true spirit of Christmas joy.

In Christmas worship the entrance sets the tone of worship. Because Christmas is a joyous and festive occasion, use music, processions, dance, choirs, and instruments to lead the people in a joyous entrance. Many churches drop the confession from the entrance because Christmas is not a time for penitence.

In the service of the word, use a dialogic reading or a drama as well as a special reference to Christmas themes in the creed and the prayers. Follow the lectionary reading to maintain biblical integrity with respect to the event being celebrated.

In the service of the table sing Communion songs that focus on the incarnation and the meaning of Christmas. Christmas carols are appropriate for singing during Communion.

THE CHRISTMAS THEME

From the very beginnings of the Christmas celebration in the early fourth century, the theme of the Christmas season has always been the arrival of the light—the light that has come to dispel darkness.

Historically, three services were celebrated on Christmas day: the midnight service, a service on Christmas morning, and another on Christmas night. The texts of these services stress the birth of Christ, but in such a way that the birth is not isolated from the death of Christ and his coming again. These themes are present in a Christmas preface prayer that states, "Grant that as we joyfully receive him for our redeemer, so may we with sure confidence behold him when he shall come to be our judge." What is at the heart of Christmas is the gospel—the overthrow of evil and the establishment of God's reign in our lives and over a restored creation.

What we are called to remember as we construct Christmas services is that Christmas is clearly a celebration of redemption. The prayers, antiphons, Scripture readings, and hymns for Christmas point us to the source of our redemption, namely, the paschal mystery in which the incarnation finds its ultimate meaning. This is clearly announced in the epistle reading for Christmas Eve: "Jesus Christ . . . gave himself for us to redeem us from all iniquity and to purify himself a people of his own who are zealous for good deeds" (Titus 2:13–14 RSV).

Christmas worship is not confined to a single day but extends for twelve days. The origin for these twelve days of festivity lies in the early church.

The early Christians of the East celebrated the birth of Christ on January 6. They transformed a pagan celebration of a god's birth on this date to a celebration of the birth of Jesus, since the date of Jesus' birth is not known. In the West, Christians began to celebrate Christmas on December 25. They converted the pagan festival of the invincible sun into the birth of Jesus. Eventually these two dates formed the boundaries of the Christmas season, with the celebration of the birth of Jesus on December 25 representing the beginning of the festival and the celebration of the manifestation of Christ to the world through the visit of the Magi on January 6 (Epiphany) representing the end of the Christmas festival.

THE TWELVE DAYS OF CHRISTMAS

We are all familiar with the twelve days of Christmas from the song "The Twelve Days of Christmas." The twelve days begin on December 25 and end on January 6. These days are inextricably linked together in one continuous celebration of the birth of Christ. All services of worship during these twelve days focus on the birth of Jesus.

CONCLUSION

Christmas is a great time of joy, a joy worth waiting for. Our longing builds through Advent, as children long for the moment to open their presents. This joy continues in our private devotion and in the worship of the assembled church, culminating in the Epiphany service of January 6 (or the nearest Sunday).

STUDY GUIDE

Read Session 3, "Joy to the World,"
before starting the study guide.

PART I: PERSONAL STUDY

Complete the following questions individually.

1. *Life Connection*
- In this lesson we want to get in touch with our experience of Christmas. Start by describing the traditions your family kept during Christmas when you were a child. _____

   _____

   _____

   _____

   _____

2. *Thought Questions*
- Explain how Matthew and Luke differ in theme regarding the birth of Christ.
   Matthew: _____

   _____

   Luke: _____

   _____

- Read the Magnificat (Luke 1:46–55). How does Mary's song express Luke's theme of Christmas? _____

   _____

   _____

   _____

   _____

   _____

   _____

   _____

- How may each part of worship during the Christmas season express Christmas joy?

  Entrance _____

  _____

  Word_____

  _____

  Table _____

  _____

  Dismissal _____

  _____

- Use your own words to express the theme of Christmas. _____

  _____

  _____

- Read Titus 2:13–14. How does this Scripture capture the essence of Christmas worship? _____

  _____

  _____

- How did the celebration of Christmas arise in the early church?

  _____

  _____

  _____

  _____

3. *Application*

- Would you say that your personal approach to Christmas emphasizes Matthew's or Luke's theme? Explain. _____

  _____

  _____

  _____

  _____

  _____

  _____

PART II: GROUP DISCUSSION

The following questions are designed for group discussion. Share the insights you gained from your personal study in Part I.

Write out all answers that group members give to the questions on a chalkboard, a flip chart, or a dry erase board.

1. *Life Connection*

♦ Begin your group discussion by asking people to share their memories of Christmas. For example, what special traditions did their families follow?

2. *Thought Questions*

♦ Compare Matthew's and Luke's themes of Christmas. Ask, "How many people identify with Matthew? How many with Luke? What can we learn about Christmas from each author?"

♦ Read through the Magnificat (Luke 1:46–55). Ask how Mary views the birth of Christ (discuss each phrase). When you have finished the discussion, sing the Magnificat. If you don't have the music, improvise.

♦ What is the theme of worship during Christmas?

♦ How can the joy of Christmas worship be expressed in the fourfold pattern of worship—the gathering, the word, the eucharist, the sending forth? Open this question for general discussion and walk through each part of worship.

♦ Does it bother you that Christmas day replaces a pagan festival to the sun god? Do you think this is a wise approach to missionary activity that should be used today?

3. *Application*

♦ Does your church celebrate Christmas according to Matthew's or Luke's approach?

♦ Get records (bulletins) of the worship of your church in the last Christmas season. Evaluate the entrance, the word, the table, and the dismissal. What evidences of the Christmas theme do you find in the service?

- Plan a Christmas worship for the next season. What texts and hymns or songs will you use to express the joy of Christmas?
- Evaluate the service you have planned. What kind of spiritual experience does it order?

THE LIGHT OF THE WORLD

A Study in Epiphany

 We are all fascinated by the images of light and darkness. And most of us have had the experience of being in the dark and finding hope in a glimmer of light.

As an adolescent I lived in Montgomeryville, Pennsylvania, in the Baptist church parsonage. Behind our house ran a small creek lined by a row of thick trees. In front of the creek, at the end of our yard, was a chicken coop. On a dark night and against the background of those trees, the coop was in total darkness. Sometimes I was sent to the coop to gather eggs when it was dark. Because I was afraid of the dark, I always insisted "only if you leave the back light of the porch burning bright." I remember how scared I was walking away from the porch into the blackness of the night. And I can recall what a relief it was coming back toward the light at the end of my walk. Epiphany is that light that shines in the darkness.

In the cycle of light we have been celebrating the hope for the light in Advent, the arrival of the light at Christmas. In Epiphany we celebrate the realization that this light shines so brightly that it covers the earth!

THE BIBLICAL BASIS FOR EPIPHANY

The word *epiphany* comes from a Greek word that means "manifestation" or "appearance."

The early church associated Epiphany with the story of the wise men who made a long journey to see Jesus, "the king of the Jews" (see Matt 2:1–12).

Many churches incorporate the journey of the Magi into their Christmas pageantry even though the event occurred months after the birth of Christ.

The significance of the wise men who came to see Jesus is found primarily in the fact that they were Gentile, not Jewish. The fact that they worshiped Jesus and that their worship was received by him has always stood as the symbol of the universal nature of Christ's mission to the world. God became incarnate not only to be the Messiah but also to be the Savior of the world. And it is in this event that Jesus is first "manifested" to the world as God's work of salvation to the whole world. Epiphany, which always occurs on January 6, represents the end of the cycle of light, or what we also call the Christmas season of worship. (January 6 does not always fall on a Sunday. Therefore, some congregations celebrate Epiphany worship on January 6, while others celebrate an Epiphany service on the Sunday that is closest to it.)

EPIPHANY WORSHIP

What kind of worship would you celebrate on Epiphany? This traditional prayer for Epiphany worship will help us find an appropriate focus:

> O God, by the leading of the star you manifested your only Son to the Peoples of the earth: Lead us, who know you now by faith, to your presence, where we may see your glory face to face; through Jesus Christ our Lord, who lives and reigns with you and the Holy Spirit, one God, now and forever. Amen. (Episcopal Book of Common Prayer)

This prayer asks that Jesus Christ, who was manifested *then*, be manifested to us *now*.

The texts for the Epiphany service express the theme announced in the opening prayer:

- Isaiah 60:1–6 speaks of the glory of God and how all nations will come to the light.
- Psalm 72:1–7, 10–14 speaks of how all the kings of the earth will pay tribute to the royal son.
- Ephesians 3:1–12 reveals God's plan for the peoples of the world.
- Matthew 2:1–12 describes the visit of the Magi to Christ.

To this prayer and these texts join songs of Christmas joy, Christmas and Epiphany banners, a great procession and recession. In other words, pull out all the stops and end the Christmas season with a powerful and celebrative worship!

WORSHIP IN THE AFTER EPIPHANY SEASON

The weeks that stretch out between January 6 and the beginning of Lent on Ash Wednesday are called the season after Epiphany.

During this season the church follows the series of manifestations of Jesus as the Christ, beginning with the baptism of Jesus and ending with the transfiguration. In each of these manifestations we learn more about Jesus and his mission to the world. The length of the season is based on the date of Easter. If Easter is early, then the Epiphany season is shortened. If Easter is late, then the Epiphany season is lengthened, to as many as eight Sundays. The after Epiphany season dwells on the manifestation of Jesus as the Christ, as shown in the gospel lectionary readings for Year A of the 3-year cycle. Think about these stories and what each one manifests about Jesus:

First Sunday	Matthew 3:13–17	The baptism of Jesus
Second Sunday	John 1:29–42	"Behold the Lamb of God"
Third Sunday	Matthew 4:12–23	"Come, follow me"
Fourth Sunday	Matthew 5:1–12	Sermon on the Mount
Fifth Sunday	Matthew 5:13–20	You are the salt and the light
Sixth Sunday	Matthew 5:21–26	Teaching about the law
Seventh Sunday	Matthew 5:27–37	Teaching about adultery
Eighth Sunday	Matthew 6:24–34	Teaching about possessions
Transfiguration	Matthew 7:1–9	The manifestation of Jesus as the Son of God

These passages all point to the manifestations of Jesus, who came to be the light of the world.

CONCLUSION

The Christian year can order and organize a congregation's spiritual pilgrimage. In Epiphany and the season after Epiphany we can see how Christ is manifested to us as the Savior of the world. This manifestation in turn calls us to be witnesses of Christ and to manifest Jesus in our lives and to others through our words and deeds. We can help those who are headed into darkness by showing them the light—the true light of the world.

STUDY GUIDE

*Read Session 4, "The Light of the World,"
before starting the study guide.*

PART I: PERSONAL STUDY

Complete the following questions individually.

1. *Life Connection*

◆ Get in touch with feelings you have had about the darkness. If there is a
   vivid story in your background of being in the dark and longing for light,
   relate it. _____

   _____

   _____

   _____

   _____

2. *Thought Questions*

◆ What does the word *epiphany* mean? _____

   _____

   _____

   _____

◆ Reflect on the Epiphany prayer, especially the petition "Lead us, who know
   you now by faith, to your presence, where we may see your glory face to
   face." How does this petition speak to the spiritual goal of Epiphany?

◆ Read and study the texts of the Epiphany service: Isaiah 60:1–6; Psalm
   72:1–7, 10–14; Ephesians 3:1–12; Matthew 2:1–12. As you read these
   texts, listen for something arising within you that could be used in an
   Epiphany worship: a song, a prayer, the idea for a sermon, a drama, a banner, or environmental art? Use the space below to record a summary of
   what comes to your mind and your heart: _____

   _____

   _____

   _____

- On each Sunday in Epiphany Jesus is manifested in a different way. Look at two or more of the following texts and note how each text manifests Christ *to you!*

Matthew 3:13–17 _____

_____

John 1:29–42 _____

_____

Matthew 4:12–23 _____

_____

Matthew 5:1–12 _____

_____

Matthew 5:13–20 _____

_____

Matthew 5:21–26 _____

_____

Matthew 5:27–37 _____

_____

Matthew 6:24–34 _____

_____

Matthew 7:1–9 _____

_____

3. *Application*

- What is the most important teaching in the Epiphany texts about your relationship to God? _____

_____

_____

_____

_____

_____

_____

_____

PART II: GROUP DISCUSSION

The following questions are designed for group discussion. Share the insights you gained from your personal study in Part I.

Write out all answers that group members give to the questions on a chalkboard, a flip chart, or a dry erase board.

1. *Life Connection*
   - Begin your discussion by asking several people to relate stories of their experience of the dark.

2. *Thought Questions*
   - Ask, "How many of you knew before reading the text the meaning of the word 'epiphany'?"
   - Discuss the Epiphany prayer. Ask, "Did anyone have an epiphany while studying this lesson?"
   - Read through the texts of the Epiphany service: Isaiah 60:1–6; Psalm 72:1–7, 10–14; Ephesians 3:1–2; Matthew 2:1–12. Ask each member of the class to share his or her creative work (song, sermon, banner, drama, etc.) for an Epiphany service. (Take time to give all group members an opportunity to share their work.)
   - Go through as many of the Epiphany gospel texts as time permits, asking two questions of each: What was manifested to the people of Jesus' time? What is manifested to us today?

Matthew 3:13–17	Matthew 5:21–26
John 1:29–42	Matthew 5:27–37
Matthew 4:12–23	Matthew 6:24–34
Matthew 5:1–12	Matthew 7:1–9
Matthew 5:13–20	

3. *Application*

• Make an application of Epiphany to your church worship. Reflect on the texts for the Epiphany service (January 6) and talk about how each person's creative idea could be used in this worship service.

• Apply Epiphany to each person's spiritual journey. Ask, "How has the Christian faith been more clearly manifested to you through these texts? How can you go forth to manifest Christ to others?"

PART II

~GGG~

THE CYCLE

OF LIFE

WALKING WITH JESUS

A Study in Lent

 I don't know about you, but I always seem to be preparing for something—a course, a lecture, a trip.

While this kind of preparation goes on all the time in my life, I've also noticed that my wife and I go through a special kind of preparation for having friends over for special celebrations such as birthdays or Thanksgiving or Christmas.

I am convinced that preparation is the key to a successful event. When a special event is prepared haphazardly or hurriedly, it doesn't seem to have much impact. This is especially true for Easter.

Lent is all about Easter preparation. When we follow Lent for six and a half weeks, Easter becomes a genuine personal experience of the resurrection.

THE BIBLICAL BASIS OF LENT

The Scriptures, of course, do not prescribe Lent. Nevertheless, the theme of Lent is drawn from Scripture. Nor does the word *Lent* have a biblical meaning. It means spring and originates from the lengthening of days as spring approaches.

The theme of Lent is spiritual preparation for Easter symbolized by the three spiritual disciplines of prayer, fasting, and almsgiving. These are disciplines that are to be done with intentionality rather than in a perfunctory or ritualistic manner.

The spiritual preparation of Lent has a special aim—entering into the death of Jesus so that the resurrection to new life may be a truly physical experience, not just an intellectual meditation.

The three disciplines, which a Christian may engage in all year long, are to be intensified during Lent. A person who truly takes up the Lenten discipline will spend more time in Scripture study and prayer and will give more for the needs of others. Through self-denial the Christian pilgrim enters into the suffering of Jesus and prepares for the resurrection.

For some people the Lenten discipline has degenerated into fasting for the sake of losing weight. For them the true meaning of Lent and the Lenten discipline is lost.

WORSHIP DURING LENT

Because Lent is the major penitential season of the Christian year, the worship of the church is more subdued, more penitential, more reflective than usual.

For example, the gathering, which is normally a time of great joy, may reflect the penitential mood by a more intense use of confession. In one church, worship begins with a silent procession during Lent. In another church, the minister, after processing, lies prostrate on the floor at the front of the church for a short time and then stands to lead the congregation in a prayer of confession. This action and prayer dramatically point to the nature of the season (in contrast to Christmas and Easter) and invoke a sense of pensive meditation.

The service of the word is also dominated by the themes of Lent: repentance, renewal, discipline. For example, here are the gospel readings for Lent from year B of the lectionary. Note the emphasis of each lesson.

Ash Wednesday	Matthew 6:1–6, 16–21	Teaching on charity, prayer, and fasting
First Sunday	Mark 1:9–13	Jesus preaches repentance
Second Sunday	Mark 8:31–38	Deny yourself and take up your cross
Third Sunday	John 2:13–22	Cleansing of the temple and foretelling of the passion
Fourth Sunday	John 6:4–15	God sent the Son not to condemn but to save
Fifth Sunday	John 12:20–33	Final hour: the Son of Man to be glorified

These Scriptures lead the congregation into an intense reflection on their relationship with Jesus.

The prayers of the eucharist do not change during Lent, but the Communion songs may shift toward a penitential emphasis and focus more on the death of Christ. This is in stark contrast to what the church will experience during Easter, when the Communion songs will focus on the resurrection and the experience of new life in Christ.

Churches that do not celebrate the eucharist weekly can adopt the alternative time of thanksgiving. They too can experience a shift of tone by expressing penitence and renewal in the time of praise and worship singing.

The dismissal generally does not change.

THE WORSHIP ENVIRONMENT OF LENT

Churches that express the season of the year in their worship environment will find much to change during Lent. Purple, the color of repentance, may be reflected in vestments, banners, the pulpit, and table hangings.

The church is quite bare during Lent. Many churches substitute a stark branch for flowers. Some branches can actually begin to sprout buds during Lent and reach an expression of life by the time Lent is nearly over. This gives the image of the life that is to come in the resurrection.

CONCLUSION

The Christian year allows for a considerable variety in worship. Some churches change the order of worship frequently, but many churches recognize that following the saving events of Jesus in the Christian year provides them with a spiritually driven variety in the experience of living, dying, and being raised to new life as the Christian year follows the pattern of the birth, life, and death of Jesus. In this way Lent allows us to experience a journey into Christ's death.

STUDY GUIDE

Read Session 5, "Walking with Jesus,"
before starting the study guide.

PART I: PERSONAL STUDY

Complete the following questions individually.

1. *Life Connection*

♦ Recall a significant event in your life this past year. How did you prepare
   for that event? _____

   _____

   _____

   _____

   _____

♦ How did your preparations for the event described above make the event
   itself enjoyable? _____

   _____

   _____

   _____

   _____

2. *Content Questions*

♦ What is the meaning of the word *Lent*? _____

   _____

   _____

   _____

♦ What is the theme of Lent? _____

   _____

   _____

   _____

   _____

◆ What are the three spiritual disciplines of Lent?

a. _____

b. _____

c. _____

◆ What is the special aim of these three disciplines? _____

_____

_____

_____

_____

◆ How can you avoid making Lent an empty and useless experience?

_____

_____

_____

_____

◆ Because Lent is a penitential season, the theme of penitence is reflected in worship. Briefly describe how each of these parts of worship may reflect that focus.

The gathering _____

_____

_____

_____

The word _____

_____

_____

_____

The eucharist_____

_____

_____

_____

The alternative time of thanksgiving _____

_____

_____

_____

- Look at each of the following gospel readings for Lent. How does each reflect the penitential theme of Lent?
  Matthew 6:1–6, 16–21 _____
  _____
  _____

  Mark 1:9–13 _____
  _____
  _____

  Mark 8:31–38 _____
  _____
  _____

  John 2:13–22 _____
  _____
  _____

  John 6:4–15 _____
  _____
  _____

  John 12:20–33 _____
  _____
  _____

- What changes can be made in the worship environment to reflect the more penitential theme of Lent? _____
  _____
  _____
  _____
  _____

3. *Application*
- Start thinking about the next Lenten season. What specific steps will you take to prepare for Easter? _____
  _____
  _____
  _____
  _____

PART II: GROUP DISCUSSION

The following questions are designed for group discussion. Share the insights you gained from your personal study in Part I.

Write out all answers that group members give to the questions on a chalkboard, a flip chart, or a dry erase board.

1. *Life Connection*

 ◆ Begin your discussion by having people talk about the preparations they made for a specific event in their life.

 ◆ Then ask people to relate how the preparation made a significant difference in their experience of the event (relate this to Lent as preparation for Easter).

2. *Thought Questions*

 ◆ Review the following basic questions about Lent:
 The meaning of the word *Lent*
 The theme of Lent
 The disciplines of Lent
 The special aim of the Lent disciplines

 ◆ If you simply follow the rules without putting your heart into Lent, you can lose its meaning. What can you do to hold onto the spiritual meaning of Lent?

 ◆ Explore how the theme of preparation for Easter may be reflected in the following parts of worship: the gathering; the word; the eucharist; the alternative time of thanksgiving.

 ◆ Read one or more of the following gospel readings appointed for Lent and comment on how each lesson encourages spiritual preparation.

> Matthew 6:1–6, 16–21   John 6:4–15
> Mark 1:9–13   John 12:20–33
> Mark 8:31–38   John 2:13–22

- How can we change our worship environment to express the theme of spiritual preparation?

3. *Application*

- How can the Lenten spiritual pilgrimage be introduced to your congregation?

- What specific spiritual renewal activities would you develop for a Lenten preparation for Easter (retreats, study groups, etc.)?

- What has this lesson taught you about Lent?

SIGN OF REPENTANCE

A Study in Ash Wednesday

 We tend to take for granted the signs and symbols that guide our lives.

Because of my travels, I'm always looking for a sign, a direction, a marker of some sort. I drive down highways looking this way and that way. Have I missed my turn? Did I get the wrong directions? Then I see it. What a relief! Signs are wonderful because they point, they lead, they direct. Because of signs we are not left to guess.

The church has always had signs. One of the most important signs of the church is the cross. In the early days of the church, new Christians were signed with the cross and told that the cross was an invisible tattoo (many people in the Roman era wore tattoos symbolizing their vocation). The vocation of the one wearing the invisible cross was to follow Jesus. Another powerful biblical symbol is ashes, which symbolize repentance. These two symbols, cross and ashes, mark the beginning of Lent and signal a time of intense spiritual reflection and renewal. The cross and ashes order our Lenten spirituality and compel us to spiritual attention.

THE BIBLICAL BASIS FOR ASH WEDNESDAY

The Scriptures do not prescribe the keeping of Ash Wednesday. But there are signs in Scripture that are used on Ash Wednesday, signs that guide our spiritual pilgrimage during Lent.

The first is the sign of the cross. No one knows the exact origin of the sign of the cross, but it goes back to the early church and frequently expresses the self-denial that is associated with Jesus. Consequently, in the early church the sign of the cross accompanied sacred actions, such as baptism. Baptism, like the cross, is the way of death, the way of negation. What is brought to death is the old life, the old way, the influence of the powers of evil. So the sign of the cross, used in the Ash

Wednesday service, symbolizes (negatively) a willingness to put to death a life lived after the flesh, and (positively) a willingness to follow Jesus, even to death.

The second sign of Ash Wednesday is the ash placed on the forehead (configured into the sign of the cross). In the Scripture, ashes are a sign of repentance. When Daniel discovered the impending desolation of Jerusalem, he "turned to the Lord God and pleaded with him in prayer and petition, in fasting, and in sackcloth and ashes" (Dan 9:3; see also 2 Sam 13:19; Job 42:6; Esth 4:1).

As you can see, ashes and the sign of the cross are two powerful symbols of repentance and intention to walk with Jesus that call us to spiritual attention.

ASH WEDNESDAY WORSHIP

What follows is an Ash Wednesday service. The text is taken from the *Book of Common Prayer*. Read through this service prayerfully as a way of reflecting on the meaning of Lent.

[A silent procession takes place. The leaders of worship are dressed in black. They may lie prostrate on the floor as a symbol of repentance. Then they may stand, and the celebrant says the following prayer:]

Let us pray.

Almighty and everlasting God, you hate nothing you have made and forgive the sins of all who are penitent: Create and make in us new and contrite hearts, that we, worthily lamenting our sins and acknowledging our wretchedness, may obtain of you, the God of all mercy, perfect remission and forgiveness; through Jesus Christ our Lord, who lives and reigns with you and the Holy Spirit, one God for ever and ever. *Amen.*

[The following Scriptures are then read:]

Old Testament   Joel 2:1–2, 12–17,   *or* Isaiah 58:1–12

Psalm   103,   *or* 103:8–14

Epistle   2 Corinthians 5:20b–6:10

Gospel   Matthew 6:1–6, 16–21

[A sermon reflecting on the Scriptures is given.]

After the Sermon, all stand, and the Celebrant or Minister appointed *invites the people to the observance of a holy Lent, saying*

Dear People of God: The first Christians observed with great devotion the days of our Lord's passion and resurrection, and it became the custom of the Church to prepare for them by a season of penitence and fasting. This season of Lent provided a time in which converts to the faith were prepared for Holy Baptism. It was also a time when those who, because of notorious sins, had been separated from the body of the faithful were reconciled by penitence and forgiveness, and restored to the fellowship of the Church. Thereby, the whole congregation was put in mind of the message of pardon and absolution set forth in the Gospel of our Savior, and of the need which all Christians continually have to renew their repentance and faith.

I invite you, therefore, in the name of the Church, to the observance of a holy Lent, by self-examination and repentance; by prayer, fasting, and self-denial; and by reading and meditating on God's holy Word. And, to make a right beginning of repentance, and as a mark of our mortal nature, let us now kneel before the Lord, our maker and redeemer.

Silence is then kept for a time, all kneeling.

If ashes are to be imposed, the Celebrant says the following prayer

Almighty God, you have created us out of the dust of the earth: Grant that these ashes may be to us a sign of our mortality and penitence, that we may remember that it is only by your gracious gift that we are given everlasting life; through Jesus Christ our Savior. Amen.

The ashes are imposed with the following words

Remember that you are dust, and to dust you shall return.

After ashes have been imposed, the service may continue with the unison reading of Psalm 51 and a litany of repentance (see the *Book of Common Prayer*, pp. 266–69). The eucharist may follow. The service concludes with a benediction and a silent recession.

Conclusion

The symbol of ashes, together with the sign of the cross, points to the way of Lent. All who receive these symbols with an open heart and intention will not lose their way during Lent. Lent will be a time of spiritual invigoration and renewal.

STUDY GUIDE

Read Session 6, "Sign of Repentance,"
before starting the study guide.

PART I: PERSONAL STUDY

Complete the following questions individually.

1. *Life Connection*

- Have you ever had the experience of being lost on the highway (or some-where else) and frantically looking for a sign to give you direction? Re-member the incident and record it. _____

_____

_____

_____

_____

_____

2. *Content Questions*

- What is the biblical meaning of the two signs used in the Ash Wednesday service?
The cross _____

_____

_____

Ashes _____

_____

_____

- What is symbolized by bringing together the cross and the ashes as the major symbols of Ash Wednesday? _____

_____

_____

_____

_____

_____

- What is your personal response to a silent procession with readers dressed in black and lying momentarily prostrate on the floor?

  _____

  _____

  _____

  _____

- Reflect on the words of the opening prayer that indicate the *need* for repentance. Look them up in the dictionary and summarize the meaning of each:

  Contrite hearts _____

  _____

  Lamenting our sins _____

  _____

  Acknowledging our *wretchedness* _____

  _____

- Look up each of the following Scriptures. How do they express the condition expressed in the words above?

  Joel 2:1–2, 12–17 _____

  _____

  Isaiah 58:1–12 _____

  _____

  Psalm 103 _____

  _____

  2 Corinthians 5:20b–6:10 _____

  _____

  Matthew 6:1–6, 16–21 _____

  _____

- Study the prayer used just before ashes are placed on the head of the worshiper. What is the dual purpose of the ashes?

  a. _____

  _____

  b. _____

  _____

  _____

3. *Application*

◆ Reflect on the words, "Remember that you are dust, and to dust your shall return." How do these words speak to you? Record your response.

_____

_____

_____

_____

_____

PART II: GROUP DISCUSSION

The following questions are designed for group discussion. Share the insights you gained from your personal study in Part I.

Write out all answers that group members give to the questions on a chalkboard, a flip chart, or a dry erase board.

1. *Life Connection*
Begin your discussion by asking several people to recall instances of being lost and finding direction in a sign.

2. *Content Questions*

◆ Review the meaning of the two signs used in the Ash Wednesday service: the cross and ashes. Ask several people to reflect on an experience of these symbols in an Ash Wednesday service in which they participated.

◆ Inquire how this group would respond to worship leaders being dressed in black and lying prostrate on the floor.

◆ Review the meaning of the following words and phrases. Ask for various insights.
Contrite hearts

Lamenting our sins

Acknowledging our *wickedness*

◆ Discuss the penitential and renewing character of each of the following Scriptures. Ask, "What does this text say to us about our disposition toward God?"
Joel 2:1–2, 12–17

Isaiah 58:1–12

Psalm 103

2 Corinthians 5:20b–6:10

Matthew 6:1–16, 16–21

◆ Read and discuss the invitation to the observance of Lent. Ask people to present the words or phrases that struck them most vividly and explain why.

◆ Review the prayer said before ashes are imposed on the head of the worshiper. Ask, "Has any here *experienced* the goal of this prayer? Explain it."

3. *Application*

◆ Review the worship of this church last year on Ash Wednesday. Ask, "What would you like to do next year?"

◆ Begin now to plan an Ash Wednesday service. What would it look like?

◆ How can you keep the Ash Wednesday service from becoming a mere ritual?

◆ What is the one most important lesson you have learned from this session?

THE DEFINING WEEK

A *Study in Holy Week*

 I wonder if you have a defining week in your calendar. I do. Let me tell you about it.

As I'm writing this manuscript, it is mid-June. My goal is to finish by the first week in August because that week is a defining week for me. It's "Webber Week" in our household, a week when the entire family gathers in Michigan on the shores of Lake Michigan for a week of beach, water sports, cookouts, and fun. After "Webber Week" I have three weeks to read, relax, and get ready for the fall when school starts.

I'm sure you have a defining week—a week that is a turning point in time. I don't mean to compare my week or your week with the final week in the life of Christ. But I do want us to sense how Holy Week ranks as *the* defining week of the entire year in the Christian's calendar. Even Christmas finds its ultimate meaning in this the week of all weeks.

THE BIBLICAL BASIS FOR HOLY WEEK

In the church of the first centuries after Christ, every Sunday was a "little Easter." Weekly worship was a special event in which the living, dying, and rising of Christ was not only told in words, but acted out in a participatory drama (the Lord's Supper).

The earliest evidence of an Easter celebration in the New Testament is found in the words of Paul written to the Corinthian community about AD 55: "Christ, our Passover lamb, has been sacrificed" (1 Cor 5:7). The clue to how Easter may have been celebrated in the primitive Christian community is found in the word *Passover*, for the earliest Christians were Jews.

Jewish worship passed on two emphases to early Christian worship. First, worship was rooted in an event. The Passover service, for example, celebrated the Exodus, when God brought the Israelites out of Egypt and made them the chosen people. Second, celebrating that event in worship made it contemporaneous—the original power of that event evoked feelings among contemporary worshipers that were similar to the ones felt by the original participants in the event. The event was celebrated and made contemporary by telling the story and acting it out.

Nevertheless, we have no actual record of an Easter service or Holy Week in the New Testament. For this we must turn to the early church.

HOLY WEEK IN THE EARLY CHURCH

Perhaps the best insight into Easter worship as story told and acted out comes from the writing of a woman named Egeria. Her *Diary of a Pilgrimage* contains a firsthand account of Easter in Jerusalem in the late fourth century. The diary, together with liturgies from that period, provides us with an inspiring picture of Easter in the early church.

According to Egeria, what we call Holy Week was known as the "great week" in fourth-century Jerusalem. This week was the most extraordinary week in the Christian calendar. It encompassed the arrest, conviction, crucifixion, death, burial, and resurrection of Christ. It was a week in which the world was redeemed—a week in which the re-creation of the world began.

Egeria describes the day-to-day events of the great week. On *Palm Sunday* all the Christians assembled at the tomb on the Mount of Olives. Carrying palms and branches in their hands, they walked slowly to the church in Jerusalem crying, "Blessed is he who comes in the name of the Lord." (The bishop of Jerusalem, symbolizing Christ, was in the midst of the crowd.) When night fell, evening prayers were celebrated and concluded with a prayer in front of a cross erected for the occasion.

On *Monday* they sang hymns and antiphons and read passages from the Scriptures appropriate to that day in Holy Week. Egeria reports that these readings and songs were continually interspersed with prayers.

On *Tuesday* they did the same except for this: "The Bishop takes up the book of the Gospels, and while standing, reads the words of the Lord which are written in the Gospel according to Matthew at the place where he said, 'Take heed that no man deceive you' " (Matt 24:4).

On *Wednesday* everything was done as on Monday and Tuesday except that the bishop read a passage where Judas went to the Jews to set the price they would pay him to betray the Lord (see Matt 26:14–16; Mark 14:10–11; Luke 22:3–6). Egeria reports that "while this passage is being read, there is such moaning and groaning from among the people that no one can help being moved to tears in that moment." (This and similar comments throughout her account suggest the powerful effect that a reenactment can have on the worshipers' feelings.)

On *Thursday evening* Communion was celebrated. Then all went home to eat their last meal before Easter. Later they returned to worship all night as a way of reenacting the gospel accounts of Thursday night. According to Egira, "They continually sing hymns and antiphons and read the Scripture passages proper to the place and to the day. Between these, prayers are said."

Early on *Friday* after worshiping all night, the Christians proceeded to Gethsemane, where they read the passage describing the Lord's arrest (see Matt 26:36–56). Egeria reports that "there is such moaning and groaning with weeping from all the people that their moaning can be heard practically as far as the city." They then went to the place of the cross where the words of Pilate were read (see Matt 27:11–26; Mark 15:1–15; Luke 23:1–25; John 18:28–19:16). Then the bishop sent the crowd home to meditate, instructing them to return about the second hour so that everyone would be "on hand here so that from that hour until the sixth hour you may see the holy wood of the cross, and thus believe that it was offered for the salvation of each and every one of us."

On *Friday night* they acknowledged the cross as the instrument of salvation. A cross was placed on the table and the people passed by "touching the cross and the inscription, first with their foreheads, and then with their eyes; and after kissing the cross, they move on."

On *Saturday* worship was conducted at the third and sixth hours. After nightfall the Easter vigil was held. Although Egeria says little about this service, we know from other sources that it was a dramatic reenactment of the resurrection. It included a service of light that celebrated Christ as the light of the world and the annual baptismal service in which people were baptized into Christ's dying and rising. (The early church practice of baptism by immersion was a graphic enactment of burial and resurrection.) The glorious service that occurred on Sunday morning (after the all-night vigil) celebrated the resurrection of Christ through readings, antiphons, preaching, and the eucharist.

Consider the involvement—the total immersion in the death and resurrection of their Lord—that the worshipers must have experienced. For weeks they had prepared for this service. Throughout Holy Week they were exhausted by the intensity of following after the events in Jesus' life that led to his death. Now, after another night of vigil and anticipation, the moment of Jesus' resurrection came.

Because these people had entered the tomb with him, they were able to experience his resurrection in a way that would never happen apart from the dramatic journey they had taken.

Finally, Egeria tells us that Easter did not end on Easter day. It was followed by eight days of celebration. The worshipers' fast was over. They identified no longer with death, but with resurrection and life. For eight days the Christians gathered in festive services that were in sharp contrast to the sober preparations for the Passion. They extended the resurrection side of Easter even as fasting had prepared for the crucifixion.

CONCLUSION

The above review allows us to see how the defining week in the life of Christ became the defining week in the life of the early church.

Today, as we recover the worship of Lent defined by Ash Wednesday and culminating in the great week, our personal walk and the corporate walk of the church with Jesus will become intensified.

STUDY GUIDE

Read Session 7, "The Defining Week,"
before starting the study guide.

PART I: PERSONAL STUDY

Complete the following questions individually.

1. *Life Connection*
- Do you and your family have a "defining week"? How does this order and organize a period of your life? _____

_____

_____

_____

_____

_____

_____

_____

_____

2. *Thought Questions*
- Summarize in your own words the biblical basis for Holy Week.

_____

_____

_____

_____

_____

_____

_____

_____

_____

_____

_____

◆ Summarize in your own words how the early Christians celebrated Holy Week (according to Egira).

Palm Sunday _____

_____

Monday _____

_____

Tuesday _____

_____

Wednesday _____

_____

Maundy Thursday _____

_____

Good Friday _____

_____

Holy Saturday _____

_____

3. *Application*

◆ Recall how you personally observed Holy Week this past year. On a scale of 1–10 (with 10 as intense), how would you rate the intensity of your observance?

Comment: _____

_____

_____

_____

_____

_____

PART II: GROUP DISCUSSION

The following questions are designed for group discussion. Share the insights you gained from your personal study in Part I.

Write out all answers that group members give on a chalkboard, a flip chart, or a dry erase board.

1. *Life Connection*

◆ Begin your discussion by asking several people to talk about their "defining week." Relate their experience of a defining week to Holy Week as the defining week of the Christian faith.

2. *Thought Questions*

◆ Holy Week is a "historical recitation" of God's saving deeds in Christ. Ask the group to describe what the early church did from Palm Sunday through Holy Saturday, then compare it with the practice of your church. Make three columns: one for the days of the week, one for the early church practice, and one for "our church" practice. Spend a good deal of time making the comparison.

3. *Application*

◆ In a column, write the days of the week from Palm Sunday through Holy Saturday. Now create two more columns: "Personal Goals" and "Corporate Goals." Use the remainder of the meeting to talk about what each person could do spiritually for each day and what the church might do each day for corporate worship.

◆ What did you learn about Holy Week from this study?

HOSANNA!

A Study in Palm Sunday

I 've been reading a book entitled *Stripping the Altar.* The book is about great feasts and street festivities of the medieval era that were brought to an end by the Reformation.

In recent years we have seen a return of the Christian street parades in what is being called the "praise march." The praise march is a parade of Christians walking through the streets of a city with banners and instruments singing praise songs. The movement has become increasingly widespread in our time and occurs in several hundred cities around the world every Sunday.

What we call Palm Sunday was originally a praise march through the streets of Jerusalem hailing Jesus as the King of the Jews!

THE BIBLICAL BACKGROUND OF PALM SUNDAY

The story of Palm Sunday is recorded in all four gospels (see Matt 21:1–17; Mark 11:1–19; Luke 19:28–45; John 12:12–19). Jesus is brought into Jerusalem on a donkey as people throw palm branches before him and cry, "Hosanna!" (This word means "save!" or "deliver!")

But the same people who welcomed Jesus as their king on Sunday turned against him by Friday of the same week and cried, "Crucify him!" The chief priests added, "We have no king but Caesar" (John 19:15).

The purpose of the Palm Sunday service is to enact this experience and to allow ourselves to actually enter into the experience of welcoming Jesus and then experiencing Jesus' rejection by the crowd.

PALM SUNDAY WORSHIP DESCRIBED

The ancient tradition of worship described by Egeria has been adapted to the use and style of the modern church. Consequently some of the features described by Egeria, such as meeting outside the church, the gospel reading of the triumphant entry, the procession into the church, and the distribution of the palms, have been retained.

If possible, the service begins outside the church (or in the basement or vestibule) to symbolize the entrance of Jesus into Jerusalem through the procession.

In the preparation to worship, the people gather around the worship leaders and choir. The service begins with an appropriate greeting followed by an anthem such as "Blessed Is the King Who Comes in the Name of the Lord" (or another appropriate anthem or song). The minister then offers a prayer that is followed by the reading of the triumphant entry. Another prayer, blessing God for the event celebrated this day, is offered. Then another suitable anthem is sung, followed by the procession of the congregation into the sanctuary while singing such hymns as "All Glory, Laud, and Honor." The mood of this part of the service, like that of the people who received Jesus into Jerusalem, is one of great joy and exuberance. This spirit of enthusiasm can be expressed through a procession in which the worship leaders and the choir process around the entire sanctuary as the people sing. At the close of the procession a brief prayer concluding this part of the service is given. The people are then seated for the service of the word.

Although it is customary to read both an Old Testament lesson and an epistle, the scripture emphasis is placed on the gospel reading of the passion in the Palm Sunday service. The object is to assist the congregation in experiencing the reality of Jesus' drama of redemption. The congregation cries, "Hosanna, blessed is he who comes in the name of the Lord." But later this same congregation will cry, "Crucify him!" So on Palm Sunday the congregation of worshipers will experience their own participation in receiving Jesus gladly and then turning their backs on him. And it will be here, in the reading of the passion, that the door into Holy Week will swing open. The passion gospel may be read using different roles, allowing the congregation to be the crowd. It is customary to have the people seated during the reading of the passion and standing at the mention of Golgotha. The service then proceeds with the sermon, the creed, the prayers, the kiss of peace, and the eucharist.

TEXTS FOR PALM SUNDAY WORSHIP

The following service for Palm Sunday is taken from the *Book of Common Prayer.* Study its content to understand how a Palm Sunday service orders our spirituality into the experience of Jesus, not to replicate it. The part of the service being described is the acts of entrance.

When circumstances permit, the congregation may gather at a place apart from the church, so that all may go into the church in procession.

The branches of palm or of other trees or shrubs to be carried in the procession may be distributed to the people before the service, or after the prayer of blessing.

The following or some other suitable anthem is sung or said, the people standing

Blessed is the King who comes in the name of the Lord. *Peace in heaven and glory in the highest.*

Celebrant: Let us pray.

Assist us mercifully with your help, O Lord God of our salvation, that we may enter with joy upon the contemplation of those mighty acts, whereby you have given us life and immortality; through Jesus Christ our Lord. *Amen.*

Here a Deacon or other person appointed reads one of the following

Year A Matthew 21:1–11

Year B Mark 11:1–11a

Year C Luke 19:29–40

The Celebrant then says the following blessing

Celebrant	The Lord be with you.
People	And also with you.
Celebrant	Let us give thanks to the Lord our God.
People	It is right to give him thanks and praise.

It is right to praise you, Almighty God, for the acts of love by which you have redeemed us through your Son Jesus Christ our Lord. On this day he entered the holy city of Jerusalem in triumph, and was proclaimed as King of kings by those who spread their garments and branches of palm along his way. Let these branches be for us signs of his victory, and grant that we who bear them in his name may ever hail him as our King, and follow him in the way that leads to eternal life; who lives and reigns in glory with you and the Holy Spirit, now and forever. *Amen.*

The following or some other suitable anthem may then be sung or said

Blessed is he who comes in the name of the Lord. *Hosanna in the highest.*

The Procession

Deacon Let us go forth in peace.

People In the name of Christ. Amen.

During the procession, all hold branches in their hands, and appropriate hymns, psalms, or anthems are sung, such as the hymn "All glory, laud, and honor" and Psalm 118:19–29.

At a suitable place, the procession may halt while the following or some other appropriate Collect is said

Almighty God, whose most dear Son went not up to joy but first he suffered pain, and entered not into glory before he was crucified: Mercifully grant that we, walking in the way of the cross, may find it none other than the way of life and peace; through Jesus Christ our Lord. *Amen.*

A special feature of the service of the word is the reading of the passion.

Year A   Matthew (26:36–75) 27:1–54 (55–66)

Year B   Mark (14:32–72) 15:1–39 (40–47)

Year C   Luke (22:39–71) 23:1–49 (50–56)

In most churches the passion is read as a drama, giving parts to various readers and allowing the congregation to serve as the crowd. This is a very effective way to read the passion, particularly when the crowd shouts, "Crucify him!"

The service continues with a sermon and ends with the eucharist (or alternative thanks) and the dismissal.

CONCLUSION

In the worship of Palm Sunday we enter into the experience of the crowd that greeted Jesus enthusiastically, but soon turned their backs on him. The reenactment of Palm Sunday is not a mere historical recitation of something that happened in the distant past, but an experience now of our own off-and-on relationship with God.

STUDY GUIDE

Read Session 8, "Hosanna!"
before starting the study guide.

PART I: PERSONAL STUDY

Complete the following questions individually.

1. *Life Connection*

◆ Have you been involved in, seen on TV, or heard other people talk about
the contemporary praise march? If so, record your response to this event
below. If you have not experienced the praise march, how would you personally respond to a praise march for Jesus in your own town?

_____

_____

_____

_____

2. *Content Questions*

◆ Read the account of Palm Sunday in one of the Gospels (see Matt
21:1–17; Mark 11:1–19; Luke 19:28–45; John 12:12–19). This was obviously an emotional event. Find as many words as you can to describe the
feelings of the people and then write them out. _____

_____

_____

_____

_____

◆ Read the account of these same people rejecting Jesus (see John
19:1–16). List below all the words that expressed their rejection of Jesus.

_____

_____

_____

_____

_____

◆ Think back over the events of Palm Sunday and of Good Friday. The same crowd cried "Hosanna!" and then cried "Crucify him!" (They thought Jesus was going to overthrow the Roman government militarily. They wanted a liberator like Moses and a king like David.) Try to read the mind of Jesus. What do you think was his emotional experience (read John 17:1–26)? Describe it. _____

_____

_____

_____

◆ What is our purpose in celebrating Palm Sunday?

_____

_____

◆ Reread the section entitled "Palm Sunday Worship Described." What parts of this worship were used in your church last Palm Sunday?

_____

_____

_____

◆ Study the section "Texts for Palm Sunday Worship" and then imagine an adaptation of this service for your own church. In the space below draw a picture of how your church could accommodate a Palm Sunday procession.

- Develop a bulletin showing how you would adapt the service in this study to the entrance acts for the Palm Sunday service. How would you have your people enact the Palm Sunday experience?_____

  _____

  _____

  _____

  _____

- In the entrance acts there are three prayers. Record from each prayer words or phrases that speak of God's saving acts celebrated in Holy Week.

  a. _____

  _____

  _____

  _____

  b. _____

  _____

  _____

  _____

  c. _____

  _____

  _____

  _____

3. *Application*

- Take some time to prayerfully read and reflect on Matthew's account of the passion (see Matt 26:36–27:54). Record your feelings below.

  _____

  _____

  _____

  _____

  _____

  _____

  _____

PART II: GROUP DISCUSSION

The following questions are designed for group discussion. Share the insights you gained from your personal study in Part I.

> Write out all answers that group members give to the questions on a chalkboard, a flip chart, or a dry erase board.

1. *Life Connection*

◆ Begin your discussion by asking persons who have walked in a praise march to tell of their experience. Then discuss the possibility of having a praise march in your city.

2. *Thought Questions*

◆ Read together as a group the account of Palm Sunday recorded in Matthew 21:1–11. Choose a narrator, a Jesus voice, and a prophet voice. Allow the rest to read the portion of the text designated as crowd. Ask, "What feelings did you have as the crowd?"

◆ Now read John 19:1–16. You will need a narrator, two or three soldiers, Pilate, chief priests and officials, a crowd, a Jesus voice. After you have read the Scripture in parts, ask the participants to describe their feelings.

◆ Discuss the purpose of celebrating Palm Sunday.

3. *Application*

◆ Using a bulletin from last year's Palm Sunday service, ask, "How was the experience of Palm Sunday enacted and experienced by this congregation?"

◆ Ask members of the group to share their drawings of processional space for the Palm Sunday service. Brainstorm how the space in your church may be used to express the procession of Palm Sunday.

◆ Ask the members of the group to present the acts of entrance they have adapted (from the sample in the text) for use in your next Palm Sunday worship.

- Plan the entrance for next Palm Sunday, incorporating all the ideas and creativity of the group.

- Finally, ask various members of the group to relate the spiritual experience they had in reading and studying this lesson.

HOLY THURSDAY

A Study in Maundy Thursday

A lot of very interesting things happen in connection with food. In my workshops I refer to the Bible as a food-driven book. The comment gets a lot of laughs, and heads bob up and down in agreement.

When you stop to think about it, most of the important events in life are celebrated around food. We eat at birthdays, weddings, anniversaries, and even funerals, to name a few occasions. Some very powerful things happen as we eat together.

Our study of Maundy Thursday takes us to a meal that Jesus ate with his disciples.

THE BIBLICAL BACKGROUND

The events of Jesus' last days on earth account for a large portion of the gospels. These events, which are recorded in some detail, are enacted by the church in its worship. In the early church and now again in today's worship renewal, the final three days of Jesus on earth are called the great triduum, or the "three great days." These days, according to the ancient Jewish way of marking time, run from our Thursday evening (which in Jewish time is already Friday) to Saturday night (which in Jewish time is Sunday morning). On these three days we remember the final events of Jesus' life through which our salvation and healing have been accomplished.

The Maundy Thursday service commemorates two events that happen in the context of a meal and one event that takes place after the meal:

- The new commandment associated with foot washing. (see John 13:1–15)
- The institution of the Lord's Supper. (see Luke 22:17–20)
- Prayer in the garden of Gethsemane. (see Luke 22:39–46)

THE MEANING OF THE MAUNDY THURSDAY SERVICE

In the ancient church the service of Maundy Thursday began the great triduum, the three great days of the paschal celebration. These were days of fasting and prayer, days when the church remembered the final acts of Christ's saving work. The day gets its name from the Latin *mandatum novum* ("a new commandment," John 13:34), which became the French *mande* and the English *maunde*. A primary meaning of this service is to celebrate the giving of the new commandment to love one another, a commandment issued in the context of Jesus washing the disciples' feet. When we celebrate this service, we renew the covenant between God and ourselves, and we are made ready for his death and resurrection. The agape meal that is celebrated in the Maundy Thursday service symbolizes, as meals in the Old Testament did, the relationship we have with God.

Today, after the agape meal, the people assemble to worship. Because of the solemnity of the moment, the service is opened in silence. A silent procession of the minister and choir is followed by a prayer. These two acts constitute the entrance to worship. The people are then seated for the Scripture readings and the sermon.

After the sermon, the ceremony of the washing of the feet is conducted. In some traditions all the people of the congregation are involved in the ceremony. In other congregations the minister washes the feet of several people in the congregation. The minister may choose to wash the feet of several church leaders, representatives from among the leaders or the ages in the congregation. All that is needed is a pitcher of water, a basin, and a towel. The people, having removed their shoes, sit in a place visible to all. The minister then washes their feet as the choir and/or congregation sings suitable anthems or songs. After the washing of the feet, the service continues with the prayers of the people, followed by the Lord's Supper.

After the Last Supper, our Lord went to the garden of Gethsemane to pray while his disciples watched and prayed with him. Consequently it has been customary to have a prayer vigil after the Maunday Thursday service, extending through the night in some churches. The church may stay open, allowing people to come and go as they please, or various persons may sign up to pray at designated half hours or hours throughout the night. For those who are able to do the vigil, the tiredness of the body itself, which is often experienced through the three days, assists the spirit in experiencing to some small degree the pain and suffering of our Lord.

An Order for Maundy Thursday

Here are the various parts of the Maundy Thursday service as it is held around the world in Christian churches of nearly every denomination:

- ◆ The Agape Meal (see Luke 22:7–16). People may gather at the church or in individual homes. The food generally served consists of bread, cheeses, nuts, dried food, and drink. After the meal the people assemble in the church.
- ◆ The Worship Service. This simple service consists of gathering prayers, the reading of Scripture, the sermon, the washing of feet, and the celebration of the Lord's Supper. The church remains open for people to pray through the night.

Here is the beginning of the worship service as expressed in the *Book of Common Prayer:*

Almighty Father, whose dear Son, on the night before he suffered, instituted the Sacrament of his Body and Blood: Mercifully grant that we may receive it thankfully in remembrance of Jesus Christ our Lord, who in these holy mysteries gives us a pledge of eternal life; and who now lives and reigns with you and the Holy Spirit, one God, for ever and ever. *Amen.*

Old Testament   Exodus 12:1–14a

Psalm   78:14–20, 23–25

Epistle   1 Corinthians 11:23–26 (27–32)

Gospel   John 13:1–15, *or* Luke 22:14–30

When observed, the ceremony of the washing of feet appropriately follows the Gospel and homily.

During the ceremony, the following or other suitable anthems or songs may be sung or said.

[Minister:] The Lord Jesus, after he had supped with his disciples and had washed their feet, said to them, "Do you know what I, your Lord and Master, have done to you? I have given you an example, that you should do as I have done."

[People:] *Peace is my last gift to you, my own peace I now leave with you; peace which the world cannot give, I give to you.*

I give you a new commandment: Love one another as I have loved you.

Peace is my last gift to you, my own peace I now leave with you; peace which the world cannot give, I give to you.

By this shall the world know that you are my disciples: That you have love for one another.

The service continues with the prayers of the people, the passing of the peace, and the eucharist. After Communion the people remain in a prayerful attitude as the church is stripped of all decorations. The church will remain bare, symbolizing death, until the Easter event. After worship is over, the church may remain open all night for prayer, even as the disciples remained with Jesus until his arrest (see Luke 22:39–53).

CONCLUSION

Holy Thursday is the beginning of the end of Jesus' ministry. The events of this day are reenacted for the sake of participants' being shaped by the gospel message. A true entrance into the meaning of the day is the call to a new way of life in Jesus.

STUDY GUIDE

*Read Session 9, "Holy Thursday,"
before starting the study guide.*

PART I: PERSONAL STUDY

Complete the following questions individually.

1. *Life Connection*

♦ Recall an event such as a birthday party, a wedding, a funeral, or some
other special occasion. Describe your recollection of the food served.
How did that food enhance your conversation and the general spirit of
the event? _____

_____

_____

_____

_____

2. *Content Questions*

♦ What is the "great triduum"? _____

_____

_____

♦ What three events does Maundy Thursday commemorate?
   a. _____

_____

   b. _____

_____

   c. _____

_____

♦ What is the meaning of the word *Maundy?* _____

_____

_____

_____

◆ What is the symbol of the meal? _____

_____

_____

_____

◆ Who may have their feet washed in a Maundy Thursday service?

_____

_____

_____

_____

◆ Draw a picture of the space in your church that could be used for the washing of the feet. Include the footwasher, the basin, and the towel.

◆ Read the account of preparation for the agape meal in Luke 22:7–16. Why was this meal so important? _____

_____

_____

_____

_____

◆ Read the account of the washing of the feet recorded in John 13:1–17. What was the point of washing feet? _____

_____

_____

_____

◆ Read the account of the institution of the Lord's Supper in Luke 22:17–20. How did Jesus re-interpret the bread and wine of the Passover meal? _____

_____

_____

_____

_____

◆ Read the account of Jesus' prayer on the Mount of Olives in Luke 22:39–46. Describe Jesus' emotional state during this prayer experience. How does the knowledge of his pain affect your approach to the Maundy Thursday service? _____

_____

_____

_____

_____

◆ Plan an agape meal for your church. Would you have everyone come to the church to eat? Would you have people eat in homes? What would you feed them to provide an authentic Palestinian meal setting?

_____

_____

_____

_____

◆ Drawing from the worship service suggested in the text, plan a worship service for your church that would include the washing of feet, the institution of the Lord's Supper, and prayers during the night.

_____

_____

_____

_____

_____

_____

+ What is the purpose of reenacting these events?

  _____

  _____

  _____

  _____

3. *Application*
+ How has this study affected you spiritually? Has it moved you to worship? Decribe your experience. _____

  _____

  _____

  _____

  _____

PART II: GROUP DISCUSSION

The following questions are designed for group discussion. Share the insights you gained from your personal study in Part I.

Write out all answers that group members give to the questions on a chalkboard, a flip chart, or a dry erase board.

1. *Life Connection*
+ Begin your discussion by asking members of the group to recall an event accompanied by food. How did the food enhance their experience of the event?

2. *Thought Questions*
+ Ask if anyone in the group has experienced the "great triduum" or if anyone knows of someone who has. Talk about the experience.

+ Ask if anyone in the group has experienced a Maundy Thursday service. Talk about the experience.

+ Ask if anyone has experienced foot washing in the Maundy Thursday service (or in an Anabaptist agape meal where foot washing is practiced). Comment on the experience.

- Have members of the group share the pictures they have drawn of the church space to be used for washing feet. Discuss this space as well as their emotional and spiritual response to the washing of feet.

- Read and briefly discuss the following Scripture accounts:

  Luke 22:7–16, gathering for the agape feast
  John 13:1–17, the washing of feet
  Luke 22:17–20, the institution of the Lord's Supper
  Luke 22:39–46, the account of Jesus' prayer on the Mount of Olives

3. *Application*

- Evaluate what you did as a church last year on Maundy Thursday.

- Draw from this study to plan a Maundy Thursday service for the next Holy Week.

- Explain how the Maundy Thursday service can be more than a mere historical recitation of a past event.

THE LAST DAY

A *Study in Good Friday*

 When someone dies, family and friends frequently ask, "What was her last day like?"

There may not be much to recount about someone whose last days were spent in a coma. Other people are leading active lives when they are suddenly snatched from life to death with little warning. Loved ones treasure memories of the last moments of their active lives.

Even though Jesus knew he was going to die, it was a sudden and cataclysmic event. The signs of death were there—the growing hatred by the religious leaders of the day, the betrayal, and the arrest. But ultimately Jesus' end was sudden and violent.

Jesus' last day is recorded in detail. That's what the family of God remembers on the day called "Good Friday."

THE BIBLICAL ACCOUNT OF THE LAST DAY

The account of the last day of Jesus, culminating in his crucifixion and burial, is found in all four gospels (see Matt 26:31–27:61; Mark 14:27–15:47; Luke 22:39–23:56; John 18:1–19:42).

Generally, the church does not attempt to retrace all the steps of his last day. Instead it often celebrates one of several services on Good Friday. These are:

- ◆ The way of the cross service
- ◆ The seven last words
- ◆ The veneration of the cross
- ◆ Tenebrae

A brief survey of these services will help us grasp the spiritual enormity of the day.

THE WAY OF THE CROSS SERVICE

This service is sometimes called the "stations of the cross." It consists of a series of fourteen devotional acts based on the fourteen events from Christ's condemnation to his entombment. Originally the way of the cross service was developed in Jerusalem in what is known as the Via Dolorosa. Today, thousands of Christians flock to Israel to do the stations of the cross in the setting where the events happened. Catholic churches, as well as many other liturgical churches, have symbols of the fourteen stations in their churches. A noon service on Good Friday follows these powerful events.

Eight of the fourteen events recalled in this service are recorded in Scripture. The other six are handed down in the tradition of the early church. Here's a list of those events, along with appropriate Scripture readings:

1. Jesus is condemned to death. (John 19:1–3, 5)
2. Jesus takes up his cross. (John 19:15–17)
3. Jesus falls the first time. (Phil 2:5–11)
4. Jesus meets his afflicted mother. (Luke 2:34–35)
5. The cross is laid on Simon from Cyrene. (Matt 11:28–30; Luke 23:26)
6. A woman wipes the face of Jesus. (Isa 53:1–3)
7. Jesus falls a second time (Isa 53:4–6)
8. Jesus meets the women of Jerusalem. (Luke 23:27–28)
9. Jesus falls a third time. (Isa 53:7–9)
10. Jesus is stripped of his garment. (Luke 23:32–38)
11. Jesus is nailed to the cross. (Isa 53:10–12)
12. Jesus dies on the cross. (Luke 23:44–46)
13. Jesus is taken down from the cross. (Isa 54:4–6)
14. Jesus is laid in the tomb. (Luke 23:50–56)

THE SEVEN LAST WORDS

Protestant churches have developed a service that lasts from noon to three o'clock (the three hours Jesus was on the cross) featuring the seven last words. Often this service is ecumenical. Each participating pastor may be responsible for one of the words. Each service may consist of a hymn, prayer, or meditation on the last words and silence. Here are the seven last words:

First word	"Father, forgive them, for they do not know what they are doing." (Luke 23:34)
Second word	"I tell you the truth, today you will be with me in paradise." (Luke 23:43)
Third word	"Dear woman, here is your son," and to the disciple, "Here is your mother." (John 19:26–27)
Fourth word	"My God, my God, why have you forsaken me?" (Matt 27:46)
Fifth word	"I am thirsty." (John 19:28)
Sixth word	"It is finished." (John 19:30)
Seventh word	"Father, into your hands I commit my spirit!" (Luke 23:46)

THE VENERATION OF THE CROSS

The veneration of the cross dates back to the fourth century. The point of the service, of course, was not to worship the cross but to remember the cross as the instrument of salvation. This service has become very popular recently and has been restored in many renewed worship communities.

As presented in the *Book of Common Prayer*, the service includes prayers, readings, hymns or anthems, and personal expressions of devotion. It begins with the people assembled, silent and kneeling, as the minister and choir enter silently. The minister says, "Blessed be our God," to which the people respond, *"For ever and ever. Amen."* The minister then says:

Let us pray.

Almighty God, we pray you graciously to behold this your family, for whom our Lord Jesus Christ was willing to be betrayed, and given into the hands of sinners, and to suffer death upon the cross; who now lives and reigns with you and the Holy Spirit, one God, for ever and ever. *Amen.*

After the prayer, three appropriate passages from Scripture are read. These include:

- Isaiah 52:13–53:12, or Genesis 22:1–18, or Wisdom 2:1, 12–24
- Psalm 22:1–11 (12–21), or 40:1–14, or 69:1–23
- Hebrews 10:1–25

Next, the passion according to John is read (18:1–19:37, or the shorter passage, 19:1–37). As on Palm Sunday, different parts are often read by different persons, with the congregation taking the part of the crowd. During the reading the congregation either stands or sits; at the part where Jesus arrives at Golgotha (19:17), everyone kneels for the reast of the reading (or, if they're seated, they stand).

After the passion is completed, everyone sits and the minister preaches a sermon. Next comes a hymn—for example, "When I Survey the Wondrous Cross"—followed by a series of solemn prayers called the "bidding prayers" because each is introduced by an invitation or "bidding" to pray (see the *Book of Common Prayer,* pp. 277–81).

Among the groups traditionally prayed for are the church, the government, those who are suffering, and those who have not heard or have rejected the gospel. After each bidding, there is silence, then the minister says a prayer and the people answer "Amen." Here, for example, is the prayer for the suffering:

Gracious God, the compfort of all who sorrow, the strength of all who suffer: Let the cry of those in misery and need come to you, that they may find your mercy present with them in all their afflictions; and give us, we pray, the strength to serve them for the sake of him who suffered for us, your Son Jesus Christ our Lord. *Amen.*

THE ENTRANCE OF THE CROSS

Some churches continue the service, with the focus shifting to the cross itself. A procession brings in the cross. It may be covered with a black cloth. As the procession begins, the cross is lowered and a portion of the black cloth is removed from one arm. The cross is lifted high, and the people sing or say an appropriate hymn or anthem, such as Anthem 1 from the *Book of Common Prayer:*

We glory in your cross, O Lord,
and praise and glorify your holy resurrection;
for by virtue of your cross
joy has come to the whole world.
May God be merciful to us and bless us,
show us the light of his countenance, and come to us.
Let your ways be known upon earth,
your saving health among all nations.
Let the people praise you, O God;

let all the peoples praise you.
We glory in your cross, O Lord,
and praise and glorify your holy resurrection;
for by virtue of your cross
joy has come to the whole world.

Then the cross is carried to the middle of the church and the black covering on the other arm is removed. The cross is again lifted high as people sing or say a hymn such as Anthem 2:

We adore you, O Christ, and we bless you,
because by your holy cross you have redeemed the world.
If we have died with him, we shall also live with him;
if we endure, we shall also reign with him.
We adore you, O Christ, and we bless you,
because by your holy cross you have redeemed the world.

The cross is then carried to the front of the church. The black covering is removed from the middle. The cross is lifted high as the people sing or say a hymn such as Anthem 3.

O Savior of the world,
who by thy cross and precious blood hast redeemed us:
Save us and help us, we humbly beseech thee, O Lord.

The people are now invited to walk forward and look at the cross, touch it, kneel in prayer, or do any other appropriate action in front of the cross, the instrument of salvation. Silence may be observed or songs of the cross may be sung in unison or by the choir. After the people have completed their acts of devotion, the following closing prayer may be said:

Lord Jesus Christ, Son of the living God, we pray you to set your passion, cross, and death between your judgment and our souls, now and in the hour of our death. Give mercy and grace to the living; pardon and rest to the dead; to your holy Church peace and concord; and to us sinners everlasting life and glory; for with the Father and the Holy Spirit you live and reign, one God, now and forever. *Amen.*

TENEBRAE

The tenebrae service was developed in the twelfth century. The word itself means "darkness." The tenebrae service is ordered around the Scripture readings of Jesus' last day. The unique feature of this service is that it begins in semidarkness with a number of candles brightly lit in an obvious place. One candle is extinguished after each reading until the congregation sits in absolute darkness. After each candle snuffing, an appropriate hymn may be sung by the congregation or choir. After the final reading when people have meditated in darkness for a time, a single candle may be lit, symbolizing the resurrection. The people leave in silence. Here are the Scripture readings:

Jesus prays on the Mount of Olives.	Luke 22:39–46
Jesus is arrested.	Luke 22:47–53
Peter disowns Jesus.	Luke 22:54–62
Jesus stands before Pilate and Herod.	Luke 22:66–23:12
Jesus is sentenced.	Luke 23:13–25
Jesus is crucified.	Luke 23:26–43
Jesus dies.	Luke 23:44–46
Jesus is buried.	Luke 23:50–56

CONCLUSION

Jesus' last day on earth was filled with drama, emotion, and passion. These services should create an emotional impact so that those attending may experience Jesus' death.

No wonder this last day is called *Good* Friday. Originally the term was "God's Friday," but it translated into English as "good." It is the day on which "God was reconciling the world to himself in Christ" (2 Cor 5:19).

STUDY GUIDE

Read Session 10, "The Last Day,"
before starting the study guide.

PART I: PERSONAL STUDY

Complete the following questions individually.

1. *Life Connection*

• Can you recall the last day of a family member, a friend, or even a nationally visible person who died suddenly? Summarize the final events of that person's life: _____

_____

_____

_____

_____

_____

2. *Thought Questions*

• Read Mark's account of Jesus' last day (see Mark 14:27–15:47). Summarize those events. _____

_____

_____

_____

_____

_____

• What are the four services developed by the church to reenact the final day of Jesus?

a. _____

b. _____

c. _____

d. _____

- Use your own words to describe *the way of the cross* service.

  _____

  _____

  _____

  _____

- Use your own words to describe the service known as *the seven last words*.

  _____

  _____

  _____

  _____

- Use your own words to describe the service known as the *veneration of the cross.* _____

  _____

  _____

  _____

  _____

  _____

- Use your own words to describe the *tenebrae* service. _____

  _____

  _____

  _____

  _____

- Which of these services would you most like to see in your church next Good Friday? Write out plans for the service. _____

  _____

  _____

  _____

  _____

  _____

  _____

3. *Application*

♦ Reflect on the service you have planned. How do you think this service can move beyond mere historical recitation to become a true spiritual experience of Jesus' last day on earth?

PART II: GROUP DISCUSSION

The following questions are designed for group discussion. Share the insights you gained from your personal study in Part I.

Write out all answers that group members give to the questions on a chalkboard, a flip chart, or a dry erase board.

1. *Life Connection*

♦ Begin your discussion by asking group members to recall the events of the last day of a family member or friend. If this is too difficult, discuss the last day of a historical or a national figure. Attempt to understand the importance of last-day memories.

2. *Thought Questions*

♦ Read together Mark's account of Jesus' last day (see Mark 14:27–15:47). Read it with parts. You will need a narrator, Jesus, Peter, Judas, the crowd, a high priest, the servant girl, Pilate. (Note: the crowd may include the part of the accusers and the soldiers.)

♦ Briefly discuss and review the basic content of each of the services developed to remember Jesus' last day (the way of the cross; the seven last words; the veneration of the cross; tenebrae).

♦ Review the services proposed by members of the class.

3. *Application*

♦ Ask the group to choose one of the four services to celebrate on the next Good Friday, then plan the service.

♦ How can you prevent this service from being a mere historical recitation? How can it become for each person an experience of entering into the last day of Jesus?

HE IS RISEN!

A Study in the Great Paschal Vigil

 What I remember most about Easter from my childhood days is the Easter sunrise service.

Adjacent to the church was a large flat spread of lawns. Shortly before Easter the workmen of the church gathered to build a platform for the Easter sunrise service. Chairs, musical instruments, the choir, and the whole church were moved to this space where the Easter service began in darkness and ended at sun-up.

This church was motivated by an early-morning-service instinct, an instinct that has guided the church from its earliest days.

In a previous lesson I introduced you briefly to the great paschal vigil of the early church (see Session 7, "The Defining Week"). In this session we are going to look at that service in detail.

BIBLICAL BASIS FOR THE GREAT PASCHAL VIGIL

Throughout our study we have seen that worship is rooted in historical events, particularly the saving events of God in Jesus Christ. Worship re-presents these events. As I have mentioned before, the representation of the saving events is not merely a historical recitation, but a proclamation and enactment attended by the Holy Spirit that makes the saving and healing power of the event available to the worshiping community. This is true of the great paschal vigil, which rehearses the pivotal salvation event—the resurrection of Jesus Christ from the dead.

The biblical root of the great paschal vigil is the story of the resurrection (see Matt 28; Mark 16; Luke 24; John 20).

THE HISTORICAL DEVELOPMENT OF THE GREAT PASCHAL VIGIL

We do not know how the great paschal vigil developed in detail. The broad outline of its development is set in the context of the baptism of new believers. Let me explain.

Converts to faith passed through a two- to three-year period of Christian instruction and spiritual formation. This time culminated in the all-night vigil and the baptism and resurrection eucharist that took place Easter morning. This service, the great paschal vigil, had four parts:

1. the service of light,
2. the service of readings,
3. the service of baptism,
4. the resurrection eucharist.

Contemporary worship renewal has recovered these services from the early church. A brief introduction to each service will help us grasp how significant Easter was to the early Christians.

THE SERVICE OF LIGHT

The people assemble in the church in darkness and gather around a soon-to-be-lit light (in my first experience of the service of light, people gathered in the dark around a kettle-type charcoal grill that we could not see). At an appointed moment a fire is lit. Here is a modern version of the service, taken from the *Book of Common Prayer*.

In the darkness, fire is kindled; after which the Celebrant may address the people in these or similar words

Dear friends in Christ: On this most holy night, in which our Lord Jesus passed over from death to life, the Church invites her members, dispersed throughout the world, to gather in vigil and prayer. For this is the Passover of the Lord, in which, by hearing his Word and celebrating his Sacraments, we share in his victory over death.

The Celebrant may say the following prayer

Let us pray.

O God, through your Son you have bestowed upon your people the brightness of your light: Sanctify this new fire, and grant that in this Paschal feast we may so burn with heavenly desires, that with pure minds we may attain to the festival of everlasting light; through Jesus Christ our Lord. Amen.

The Paschal Candle is then lighted from the newly kindled fire, and the Deacon (the Celebrant if there is no deacon) bearing the Candle, leads the procession to the chancel, pausing three times and singing or saying

The light of Christ.

People Thanks be to God.

If candles have been distributed to members of the congregation, they are lighted from the Paschal Candle at this time. Other candles and lamps in the church, except for those at the Altar, may also be lighted.

The Paschal Candle is placed in its stand.

Then the Deacon, or other person appointed, standing near the Candle, sings or says the Exsultet, as follows (the indicated sections may be omitted).

Rejoice now, heavenly hosts and choirs of angels,
and let your trumpets shout Salvation
for the victory of our mighty King.
Rejoice and sing now, all the round earth,
bright with a glorious splendor,
for darkness has been vanquished by our eternal King.
Rejoice and be glad now, Mother Church,
and let your holy courts, in radiant light,
resound with the praises of your people.
All you who stand near this marvelous and holy flame,
pray with me to God the Almighty
for the grace to sing the worthy praise of this great light;
through Jesus Christ his Son our Lord,
who lives and reigns with him,
in the unity of the Holy Spirit,
one God, for ever and ever. *Amen.*

The Lord be with you.
Answer And also with you.
Deacon Let us give thanks to the Lord our God.
Answer *It is right to give him thanks and praise.*
Deacon
It is truly right and good, always and everywhere, with our whole heart and mind and voice, to praise you, the invisible, almighty, and eternal God, and your only-begotten Son, Jesus Christ our Lord; for he is the true Paschal Lamb, who at the feast of the Passover paid for us the debt of Adam's sin, and by his blood delivered your faithful people.

This is the night, when you brought our fathers, the children of Israel, out of bondage in Egypt, and led them through the Red Sea on dry land.

This is the night, when all who believe in Christ are delivered from the gloom of sin, and are restored to grace and holiness of life.

This is the night, when Christ broke the bonds of death and hell, and rose victorious from the grave.

How wonderful and beyond our knowing, O God, is your mercy and loving-kindness to us, that to redeem a slave, you gave a Son.

How holy is this night, when wickedness is put to flight, and sin is washed away. It restores innocence to the fallen, and joy to those who mourn. It casts out pride and hatred, and brings peace and concord.

How blessed is this night, when earth and heaven are joined and man is reconciled to God.

Holy Father, accept our evening sacrifice, the offering of this candle in your honor. May it shine continually to drive away all darkness. May Christ, the Morning Star who knows no setting, find it ever burning—he who gives his light to all creation, and who lives and reigns for ever and ever. Amen.

It is customary that the Paschal Candle burn at all services from Easter Day through the Day of Pentecost.

THE SERVICE OF READINGS

In the early church Christians listened to Scripture readings the entire night until the break of dawn and the baptism. The readings began in Genesis with the creation of the world and the fall and then traced salvation history through the patriarchs, Moses and Israel, David, the prophets. The story culminates in the coming of Christ and the resurrection declared in baptism and eucharist.

Today the readings are a bit shorter. The major readings are:

The story of creation	Genesis 1:1–2:2
The flood	Genesis 7:1–5, 11–18; 8:8–18; 9:8–13
The sacrifice of Isaac	Genesis 22:1–18
Israel's deliverance from the Red Sea	Exodus 14:10–15:1
God's presence in a renewed Israel	Isaiah 4:2–6
Salvation offered freely to all	Isaiah 55:1–11
A new heart and a new spirit	Ezekiel 36:24–28

| The valley of dry bones | Ezekiel 37:1–14 |
| The gathering of God's people | Zephaniah 3:12–20 |

These readings may be shortened, or additional readings may be added.

THE SERVICE OF BAPTISM

After the readings the congregation shifts into the baptismal service. Here the candidate confirms faith in the triune God and is baptized into the name of the Father, the Son, and the Holy Spirit.

In the early church, the catechumen (one being instructed) was invited for the first time to receive the bread and wine after baptism.

Today this service varies, depending on the tradition represented.

THE RESURRECTION EUCHARIST

The final part of the great paschal vigil is the eucharist.

The celebration of the resurrection is expressed best in the breaking of the bread, which is the symbol of the resurrected Christ among us (read Luke 24:1–49).

The eucharist begins with words from Luke 24:34. The minister may face the people and say, "He is risen!" And the people cry, "He is risen indeed!"

The resurrection is then greeted by the singing of the Gloria in Excelsis Deo—usually with all the instruments available to the church. In many churches, during the singing of this ancient hymn, numerous flowers are brought into the sanctuary which has been bare since Maundy Thursday. They are placed in front of the church as an expression of the return of life.

The sermon focuses on the meaning of the resurrection. The Communion songs are sung as people receive the bread and wine. They are primarily songs of victory and resurrection.

CONCLUSION

The ancient great paschal vigil was a highly dramatic and emotional experience of the resurrection. Believers had passed through six and one-half weeks of self-denial and waiting. During the final three days most people had spent their time in fasting and prayer. But now Christ was risen. Joy had returned to life. And they returned to their homes for a time of great feasting and celebration.

STUDY GUIDE

Read Session 11, "He is Risen!"
before starting the study guide.

PART I: PERSONAL STUDY

Complete the following questions individually.

1. *Life Connection*

♦ What is your earliest or best recollection of an Easter sunrise service? Summarize your experience. _____

_____

_____

_____

2. *Thought Questions*

♦ What does the great paschal vigil rehearse? _____

_____

_____

_____

♦ Read the resurrection account in Mark 16. What is the emotional content of this event? _____

_____

_____

_____

♦ What are the four parts of the ancient paschal vigil?
  a. _____
  b. _____
  c. _____
  d. _____

- Use your own words to briefly describe the service of light.

  _____
  _____
  _____
  _____

- Compare the content of the Exodus with the content of the Christ event as described in the Exsultet sung in the service of light. _____

  _____
  _____
  _____
  _____

- Summarize in your own words the service of readings. _____

  _____
  _____
  _____
  _____

- What is the significance of the service of baptism? _____

  _____
  _____
  _____
  _____

- What is the significance of the eucharist in this service?

  _____
  _____
  _____
  _____

- How does the great paschal vigil compare to the Easter service at your church? _____

  _____
  _____
  _____
  _____

3. *Application*

◆ As you reflect on the great paschal vigil, what spiritual insights do you experience? Comment. _____

_____

_____

_____

_____

PART II: GROUP DISCUSSION

The following questions are designed for group discussion. Share the insights you gained from your personal study in Part I.

Write out all answers that group members give to the questions on a chalkboard, a flip chart, or a dry erase board.

1. *Life Connection*

◆ Begin your discussion by asking various members to recall their experience of Easter worship.

◆ Ask if any group members have experienced a contemporary version of the ancient great paschal vigil. Invite them to relate the experience.

2. *Thought Questions*

◆ Read Mark 16 as a group. Discuss the emotional content of the story. Ask, "How did the account of the resurrection change the lives of Jesus' followers?"

◆ Discuss each of the four parts of the great paschal vigil by asking the following questions:

What is the message of the prayers in the service of light?

What is the message of the service of readings?

What is the significance of being baptized on the day of the resurrection?

What is the significance of celebrating the eucharist on the day of resurrection?

3. *Application*

- Plan a great paschal vigil for use in your church next year.

- How can you prevent this service from becoming a mere recitation of historical fact? How can you turn it into a true experience of the resurrection and the joy that accompanies the resurrection?

A TIME OF CELEBRATION

A Study in the Easter Season

 I grew up in a Christian tradition that did not follow the Christian year. Yes, of course, we celebrated Christmas and Easter. And, I suppose, to that extent my tradition followed the Christian year.

But truly following the Christian year, as we have seen in this study, means preparing for Christmas and Easter (Advent and Lent) and responding to Christmas and Easter (Epiphany and the Easter season).

When I was a boy, Christmas and Easter essentially came and went in a single day. In this study we are going to see that Easter, dating back to the early church and now increasingly in the contemporary church, is a season, not a day.

BIBLICAL BASIS FOR THE EASTER SEASON

The Easter season is the time between the resurrection and Pentecost. In the Scriptures, much happened during this time. (See the final chapter of each gospel and the first chapter of Acts.)

During the time between the resurrection and Pentecost Jesus met with his disciples to teach them, ate and fellowshiped with them, and ascended into the heavens. The Easter season recalls all of this and ends with Pentecost, the celebration of the coming of the Holy Spirit.

HISTORICAL VIEW OF THE EASTER SEASON

The writings of the early church fathers are full of praise for the season as an extended time to celebrate the resurrection. Here are several quotes from their writings:
- Easter is "a most joyous space." (Tertullian, c. 200)
- Easter "extends its beams, with unobscured grace, to all the Seven Weeks." (Athanasius, Bishop of Alexandria, c. 325)
- Easter "reminds us of the resurrection which we await in the other world." (Basil of Caesarea, 380)

The early church referred to the Easter season as a "week of Sundays" or the "great Sunday." In these admonitions and descriptions, we gain a glimpse of how the early church viewed and celebrated Easter. How can we recover this great sense of fulfillment and joy?

THE JOYOUS EASTER SEASON OF THE EARLY CHURCH

Three very significant factors in the early Christian communities laid the groundwork for a deeply felt experience of a joyous resurrection. They were
- the long Lenten period of fasting and self-denial, as well as the three-day preparation during Holy Week for the great paschal vigil;
- the presence of the catechumens in worship as they prepared for baptism (death to the old, resurrection to the new), serving as a living testimony to God's present saving action among them;
- the weekly celebration of the eucharist—the "little Easter" continually made the resurrection a present reality.

The early Christians made Sundays in Easter special:
- Worship was highly festive (in contrast to the more penitential nature of Lent). The emphasis was on the festive character of Christ's resurrected experience with the disciples at they *ate* together.
- Prayers were said standing. Standing is more joyous than kneeling, which is more penitential.
- Worship was full of alleluias. During Lent alleluias were not sung. The early Christians made up for it during Easter with many alleluias.
- Postbaptismal instruction to the catechumens concentrated on the mystery of baptism and the eucharist. In these actions the church experiences the resurrection. The presentation and the discussion, as well as the ensuing joy, spilled over into the congregation.

Today, there is an attempt within the church to recover the Easter *season* and the joy that characterizes it. How can we adapt what we have learned from the early church to our churches today?

THE EASTER SEASON TODAY

How can you make Easter more joyous? Look at those elements in the early church that made its Easter season powerful. Then draw from the ancient church what you can use.

For example, adapt a time of preparation for Easter that is penitential in character. Then make sure Easter worship is celebrative.

The joyous experience of Easter can be expressed in the worship of the church through joyous entrance songs, Easter theme preaching, and Easter theme Communion songs.

Singing establishes a mood. In Lent the music is downbeat and sober. In Easter the music is joyous and upbeat. For the gathering, use expressive music that is not only full of the joy of gathering but is easy to sing. In the service of the word, sing numerous alleluias, particularly before the reading of the gospel.

Preaching can also communicate joy. During Lent the preaching is more severe, calling for repentance and self-denial. The lectionary texts for Easter are much more joyous in character. They emphasize the presence of the risen Christ, the power of the Holy Spirit in us, and the new life in Christ. Be sure to emphasize the positive, fulfilling side of Christianity during the Easter season.

Then there is the eucharist. If you don't celebrate the eucharist weekly, do so during Easter. But make sure it is a joyous experience! Achieve joy in the Communion song. Sing as people come to receive the bread and wine. Sing songs that celebrate the victory of Christ over the powers of evil, songs of the resurrection, and songs of the exaltation of Christ.

CONCLUSION

The kind of worship we are talking about for the Easter season will lift the spirits of your congregation and fill them with joy. The experience of a joyous Easter will not be concocted or contrived, but generated by the spirit of worship.

STUDY GUIDE

Read Session 12, "A Time of Celebration,"
before starting the study guide.

PART I: PERSONAL STUDY

Complete the following questions individually.

1. *Life Connection*

◆ Recall the celebration of Easter in the church of your upbringing. Was Easter a day or a season that continued to the day of Pentecost? If you celebrated an Easter season, what was its content? _____

_____

_____

_____

_____

2. *Content Questions*

◆ Read Luke 24:13–53 and Acts 1:1–26. Outline the events that occurred between the resurrection and the day of Pentecost. _____

_____

_____

_____

_____

◆ The early church fathers extolled the Easter season. What do the following statements about the Easter season *mean* to you?

Tertullian: Easter is "a most joyous space."_____

_____

Athanasius: Easter "extends its beams, with unobscured grace, to all the Seven Weeks." _____

_____

_____

A "week of Sundays." _____

_____

The "great Sunday." _____

_____

- What three factors lead to the joyous nature of the Easter season?

  a. _____

  _____

  b. _____

  _____

  c. _____

  _____

- In your own words, describe the four actions used by early Christians to make the Easter season special.

  a. _____

  _____

  _____

  b. _____

  _____

  _____

  c. _____

  _____

  _____

  d. _____

  _____

  _____

- How can you express the joy of resurrection in the four parts of worship today? Comment.

  The entrance _____

  _____

  _____

  _____

  _____

- The word _____
  _____
  _____
  _____

- The eucharist _____
  _____
  _____
  _____

- The dismissal _____
  _____
  _____
  _____

3. *Application*
- How is your own spiritual life energized as you move from the penitential experience of Lent to the joyous experience of the resurrection?
  _____
  _____
  _____
  _____

PART II: GROUP DISCUSSION

The following questions are designed for group discussion. Share the insights you gained from your personal study in Part I.

Write out all answers that group members give to the questions on a chalkboard, a flip chart, or a dry erase board.

1. *Life Connection*
- Begin by asking if anyone in the group has ever truly celebrated Easter for seven weeks. Discuss the celebration and the spiritual effects it had on their lives.

2. *Thought Questions*

♦ Read Luke 24:13–53 and Acts 1:1–26. Ask, "How do you interpret what happened in the postresurrection period? Are there any clues to what Jesus taught? Are there any clues to the disciples' emotional condition during this period?"

♦ Have all group members present their interpretations of the early church fathers' statements about the Easter season.

♦ Discuss each of the three factors that lead to a joyous Easter season.

♦ Request comments on the four actions used by the early Christians to make Easter special.

♦ How can you can make each of the four parts of worship a special celebration of the resurrection during the Easter season?

3. *Application*

♦ Evaluate the services of your church in the past Easter season. How do they stack up against the suggestions made in this study?

♦ Plan a post-Easter service that retains a sense of the resurrection's power.

♦ How can you keep these services from being a mere recitation of history? How can you make them communicate the continuing power of the resurrection?

PART III

~-ഗ-ഗ-

PENTECOST

AND AFTER

LIFE GOES ON

A Study in Pentecost and After

One of the biggest events in my life was my daughter's wedding. I don't remember all the details, but preparing for that major family event seemed to go on forever.

An engagement party, showers, invitations, rehearsal, and then the big event, all followed by a few more parties. But then it was over. And life had to go on.

The festive season of Easter ends with the Pentecost service—and there are few occasions more festive than Trinity Sunday. Then the church goes into ordinary time, and worship goes on as the church proceeds toward Advent once again.

What do you do when the party is over and life goes on?

In this study we are going to look at Pentecost—the final Easter celebration—and at what the church calls "ordinary time."

PENTECOST

Pentencost Sunday is both an end and a beginning. "Every ending," someone once said, "is a new beginning." Pentecost is the end of the Easter season. Pentecost is the beginning of the season after Pentecost.

The biblical roots of Pentecost are found in Acts 2:1–47, which appropriately ends with a description of the post-Pentecost community worshiping in Jerusalem.

We all know what happened on the day of Pentecost. The Spirit who had been promised to the disciples (see John 15:26–27) now came to endow the disciples with understanding and empowerment.

In understanding they proclaimed Jesus as Messiah and Lord (see Acts 2:36).

The disciples proclaimed Christ with boldness (see Peter's sermon, Acts 2:14–36). On that day the church was manifest.

Pentecost Worship Today

It is my impression that many churches simply gloss over Pentecost day. It doesn't seem to be the feast day it was in the early church.

But worship renewalists are calling for greater attention to Pentecost day because of the significance it has in observing the end of Easter, the coming of the Holy Spirit, and the beginning of the season known as "after Pentecost." What can be done to make Pentecost special?

First, employ a special use of the arts for the gathering. The primary symbol of the day is the flame of fire (the tongues of fire that rested on the heads of the disciples, Acts 2:3). This symbol can be expressed through the color red in the vestments, banners, and decorations of the church. (I know of a church that asks everyone to wear something red to the Pentecost service.)

Second, try reading the Acts 2 account in multiple languages. People of different cultures can participate in this. One church has five people read in unison the Acts account, each in his or her native tongue.

Third, the sermon should certainly emphasize the Holy Spirit.

And last but not least, the songs of gathering and the songs of Communion may be expressive of the work of the Holy Spirit.

These simple suggestions will turn Pentecost into a festive occasion and lift into the hearts of the worshipers a clear sense of the significance of the coming of the Holy Spirit and the birth of the church.

After Pentecost

Once the festival celebrations of Advent, Christmas, Epiphany, Lent, Holy Week, Easter, and Pentecost are over, a long stretch of time known as the nonfestive season, or ordinary time, spans through the summer and fall months until the festive cycle begins again.

Ordinary time has a character that is distinctly different from that of the festal seasons, particularly in the fact that the various Sundays are not connected by a particular theme. In Advent we await the coming of Christ; during Christmas we celebrate his arrival; and at Epiphany we proclaim that Christ is manifest to the world as Savior. During Lent we prepare for his death; during Holy Week we reenact his death; then at Easter we celebrate his resurrection. We complete the Easter cycle with the celebration of the coming of the Holy Spirit. But in the nonfestive season of the church year, there is no unified theme that ties the Sundays together.

What is primary during the season after Pentecost is the simple but powerful meaning of Sunday. Every Sunday is the celebration of the death and resurrection of Jesus, the paschal mystery through which we and the world are saved. In this celebration is the promise of a restored human person and a re-created world. Because Christ dethroned the power of evil on the cross, we live in the expectancy of his ultimate triumph over evil and the redemption of the world from the kingdom of darkness.

The festive time of the church year is also rooted in the paschal mystery, but it concentrates on a certain aspect of that mystery: the longing of Israel; the incarnation of the Savior; the manifestation to the world; the expectancy of death; the events surrounding Christ's death, burial, resurrection, and ascension; and the coming of the Holy Spirit. Thus while every Sunday of the festal season does celebrate the entire paschal mystery, the seasonal themes emphasize one aspect of the whole. No such seasonal themes exist for the other half of the church year.

Nevertheless, the Communion lectionary has been laid out in such as way that sermons can move through a larger portion of Scripture in a series on a particular book of the Bible, picking up book themes. There are also certain festive days during the ordinary time.

- Trinity Sunday (first Sunday after Pentecost), Matthew 28:16–20,
- All Saint's Day (Sunday closest to November 1), Matthew 5:1–12,
- Thanksgiving day, Luke 17:11–19,
- The Feast of Christ the King (last Sunday before Advent), Luke 23:33–43.

CONCLUSION

In this course, *Rediscovering the Christian Feasts*, we have been walking with Jesus and allowing his life, ministry, death, and resurrection, as well as the birth of the church, to order our spiritual pilgrimage. We do not follow this pattern as a rote exercise, but as a real spiritual pilgrimage. In that way Christ takes up residence within us and forms us into his image.

STUDY GUIDE

Read Session 13, "Life Goes On,"
before starting the study guide.

PART I: PERSONAL STUDY

Complete the following questions individually.

1. *Life Connection*
- Remember a time when you prepared for and anticipated a great event, such as a marriage in your family or some other equally demanding experience. How did you extend the joy of the event beyond the day of the event? _____

_____

_____

_____

_____

2. *Content Questions*
- Read Acts 2:1–47. Outline the events of the day of Pentecost.

_____

_____

_____

_____

_____

_____

- Interpret the content of Peter's Pentecost sermon.

_____

_____

_____

_____

_____

_____

- Suggest some ideas to make Pentecost Sunday a more special day in the life of the church. _____
  _____
  _____
  _____
  _____

- What is the specific character of the after Pentecost season?
  _____
  _____

- What unified theme ties together each of these seasons?
  Advent _____
  Christmas _____
  Epiphany _____
  Lent _____
  Holy Week _____
  Easter _____

- How does the after Pentecost season differ from all other seasons?
  _____
  _____

- Name several festive days of the after Pentecost season.
  _____
  _____
  _____
  _____

3. Application

- Can you sum up in a word or phrase what you have learned from this session, as well as all other sessions in this study of the Christian year?
  _____
  _____
  _____
  _____

PART II: GROUP DISCUSSION

The following questions are designed for group discussion. Share the insights you gained from your personal study in Part I.

Write out all answers that group members give to the questions on a chalkboard, a flip chart, or a dry erase board.

1. *Life Connection*
- Begin your discussion by asking people to comment on how they extended the joy of a particular event past the day of the event itself.

2. *Thought Questions*
- Read Acts 2:1–47. Ask, "How do you interpret what happened on the day of Pentecost?"
- Read again Acts 2:14–36 (Peter's Pentecost sermon). Ask, "How do you interpret this sermon?"
- Read again Acts 2:42–47. Ask, "How does this passage describe worship after Pentecost?"
- Review the special character of each of the seasons of the Christian year studied in this course.
- Explore how the time after Pentecost differs from all other seasons.

3. *Application*
- How has your church made the after Pentecost experience of worship special?
- Plan a Pentecost worship.
- How has this study and the study of all the seasons of the Christian year influenced or shaped your understanding and practice?